The chronicle of an ill-fated B-24 aircrew
in WWII in the Pacific.
Trial with stone-age Malanesians and
the Japanese Kempe Tai.
Triumph in their *Fight for Survival*.

**Captain James Austin McMurria**
**U.S. Army Air Corps**

# FIGHT FOR SURVIVAL!

## An American Bomber Pilot's 1,000 Days as a P.O.W. of the Japanese

**With An Introduction By
Brigadier General Ed. Y. Hall,
USA/SCSG, Retired**

**By
Captain
James Austin McMurria,
U.S. Army Air Corps**

All photos with the exception of author's personal photos
courtesy of United States Department of Defense,
Australian National Archives, and
Australian War Memorial.

ISBN: 1-885354-24-X

This edition published by arrangement with Honoribus Press.

First Printing: April 1991
Second Printing: August 1991
Third Printing: February 1992
Fourth Printing: September 2005

Printed in the United States of America
Altman Printing Co., Inc.
Spartanburg, South Carolina

# TABLE OF CONTENTS

My crew plus a few friends.

Front row L-R: Sgt. Thompson – Tail gunner; Sgt. Walters – Radio operator; Lt. Sugden – Navigator;
Lt. Tom Doyle – Bombadier; Lt. Wynne – Nose gunner

Back row L-R: Cpl. Grondolfo – Waist gunner; Lt. Fyllin – Staff Operations; Lt. James McMurria – Pilot;
Lt. Martindale – Co-pilot; Sgt. Burnette – Engineer/gunner; Unknown – Gunner; Lt. R.O. Brown – Pilot; Passenger

# INTRODUCTION

By November 1941 America was all but at war. Aviation Cadet James McMurria was within a few months of obtaining the Silver Wings of an Army Air Corps pilot and the rank of a Second Lieutenant. Lend Lease had been in effect since March with England and Russia receiving massive aid from the United States. On war footing the U.S. Navy was patrolling in the Atlantic Ocean and assisting with the delivery of military goods to England. American merchant ships and two destroyers had already been torpedoed.

There was tension between the United States and Japan concerning their intentions with Indo-China and China. A Japanese Envoy was actually in the United States discussing the resolution of several serious issues of concern between the two nations.

War finally came with the Japanese attack on Pearl Harbor early on the morning of December 7, 1941. Simultaneously a second attack was launched against American Forces in the Philippines. The U.S. Navy Pacific Fleet was severely damaged with the loss of many ships. The Air Corps also sustained many losses of aircraft and personnel.

War was declared on Japan the next day with President Roosevelt's "Day of Infamy" declaration launching America into a World War which would soon also include war with Germany and Italy. The situation for America and her Allies was very bleak. Japanese early progress was very rapid with the invasion of the Philippines and the capture of Manila by January 2, 1942, Malaya and Singapore by February 15th, the Netherlands Indies by March 1st. The fall of Sumatra, Borneo and Java followed. Japan was already in Burma and Rangoon and was closing in on the Burma Road by March 9th.

The Japanese continued their victorious move towards Australia with a great naval victory in the Java Sea. American and Dutch losses amounted to 13 cruisers and destroyers. The Japanese steamroller appeared to be unstoppable. Their attack pressed further south in three directions: Burma, New Guinea and a preliminary drive on Australia. Bataan and Corregidor were gone by May 6th. In the meantime, 26 nations had signed the UN Pact at Washington calling for a unanimity of purpose and action against the Axis Powers. Each country pledged his country's full resources in the pursuit of the war and agreed that no separate peace was to be made.

Allied naval victories at the Battle of the Coral Sea and Midway in May and June finally slowed down the Japanese advances against Hawaii and Australia. The Japanese loss of four aircraft carriers and the cream of their crop of naval pilots was to be a major turning point in the war.

While the Japanese stumbled and slowed their movement south they were by no means stopped. Their intention was to continue movement towards Australia with their remaining forces making landings in the Solomons Islands. The Allies countered with a major landing on the Island of Guadalcanal in August which was to finally result in another reverse for the Japanese when they were unable to throw the American Force back into the sea. The Japanese had planned to use an airfield at Guadalcanal to launch major air attacks against Australia in support of a potential invasion. The fight for Guadalcanal was a bloody battle for both sides.The U.S. Army and Marines prevailed and soon the airfield was being used to protect the Allied supply line to Australia. The build up to turn the tide was underway.

In Australia, General Kenney had been put in command of the tiny Fifth Air Force by General MacArthur who had been ordered out of the Philippines by President Roosevelt to command Allied Forces in the South Pacific. The Fifth Air Force was made up of what was saved from the retreat debacle towards Australia and consisted of a real mix of fighters and bombers needing maintenance, pilots and crews. This period of the war found the Fifth Air Force barely hanging on by the skin of their teeth. The Japanese Air Force was still quite strong and a very formidable foe. The Fifth's early actions were mere pin prick attacks against Japanese convoys and ground forces operating in New Guinea and other areas of the South Pacific. Other air combat operations consisted of attacks against the major naval and supply base at Rabaul. General Kenney was begging for more air assets and finally, in October 1942, a flight of eight B-24's arrived from the United States via Hawaii. This was the leading edge of the buildup of Allied Air Forces. Enter Lieutenant James McMurria, his brand new B-24 Liberator Bomber and the 90th Bomb Group soon to become known as"The Jolley Roger's."

Lieutenant McMurria's struggle and epic fight for survival as a POW in a place called "Hell on Earth," was about to begin.

Ed.Y.Hall, Brigadier General,
USA/SCSG, Retired
Publisher, Honoribus Press

# BEGINNING OF DIARY

Diary and reflections of James A. McMurria commencing with time of graduation from Army Flying School at Brooks Field, Texas, February 20, 1942. The Ledger is actually brought up to date by a synopsis of events and happenings between February 20, 1942 and the present date, November 18, 1942, and is begun at Mareba, Australia.

∞

February 20, 1942 was a big day for me. Mother and Dad came out to San Antonio and brought Sheila Averett with them to see me get wings. Rosalind Russell presented them after an excellent pep talk. Very noticable were her lyle stockings which Sheila and Mother noticed first, strange as it seems. Took some movies of her and she graciously winked at the camera. Drove out to Gallagah's Ranch – very colorful – more movies. Didn't eat lunch until around 4 o'clock – with Sheila at La Louisiane – menu in French so the bumkins eat two steaks after a quart of champagne in a deserted restaurant.

Drove to Columbus in record-breaking time after a short stop at Natchez, Miss. – Dad checking gasoline consumption of the "Clipper" every hundred miles.

Arrived at my post McDill Field Tampa, Fla. around Feb 26th. I sincerely doubt if I'll ever be able to fly a B-17 with four motors – biggest damn thing I ever saw – played tennis and had a meal with Janet and Hollis a few days later. There are too many pilots and too few B-17's in the squadron so after around 30 hours I'm attached from the 97th Group to the Halpro Detachment which is equipped with B-24's. Here I was checked out by a colonel Feldman as first pilot after 28 hours. Getting to be hot stuff now. Enjoyed rooming with Archie Hill, an Alabama boy, and through him met a number of Tampa's cream puffs. He was a ground officer and around the last of March left McDill for flying school. The Halpro's move out for Ft. Myers, Fla. and I am ordered to join the 93d Group at Barksdale Field, La. Stopped by Columbus on the way out and saw the family and Shelia. My bosom buddy Curtis Jordan here in after refared to as Curt or Kirk, has not been drafted and I have my doubts if the lucky B--- will ever be called.

Arrived Barksdale April 4, 1942. Nice Post – Dubard and Davis whom I had known at McDill are the first persons I meet. Captain Baker is my new squadron C.O. Am not altogether satisfied with this squadron and am when we split up and form the 90th Group on May 17th. Ray Walker and Alicia, his wife have been my closest friends. They are throughly interested New Haven love birds. They both like good music and she recieves a wonderful album of records from home that is to soothe the jangled nerves quite a few evenings with the aid of round house scotch and sodas. Jeanette Sental begins to make a foursome out of it. She's the local Czarina but takes no end of beatings from our total disregard for her beauty and brains. She has plenty of both and I can't understand why she doesn't arouse me to something more than mere friendship.

Herb Frawley digs a wing into the ground around three o'clock in the morning with several demolitions on board. Sad. My work in the squadron gets confining as hell and after so much of it I bust loose with a flurry of friviolity for many nights, Jeanette being my constant companion and friend. Won second place in a putting contest on "family night" at the Shreveport Country Club. Next day took a cross country flight to New Orleans, Montgomery, Memphis and back – Dinner in the French Quarter of New Orleans. Sent a telegram from there to Jeanette asking if she wasn't a personal friend of James McMurria and could she arrange an interview signed Tommy Armour. Rumor has it that the group is leaving for Washington State so we wind up in Greenville, S.C. I drive up to Hendersonville, N.C. and see the family several times before the end of June. Shelia, fast becoming a passing fancy in my affections, throws me in contact with Mary Frances Smith of Greenville. I'm very much impressed and believe I always will be. Bombardiers and Navigators join the squadron immediately. My friends among them consist of Hardy, Doyle, Gunther and Devine. Hobson gets into bad weather and crashes about the middle of July. Mary Frances is definitely "the girl" and it seems mutual.

The Group leaves for Ypsilanti, Michigan 6 August to be stationed at Ford's Willow Run B-24 plant apparently for morale reasons. The workers in the plant have been striking too frequently. Most everyone is dissatified with living conditions and Detriot in general. Went to a dance in Ann Arbor with Patterson and Doyle and a bad time was had by all. I soon cook up business in Greenville and make it necessary to return. Miss Smith becomes increasingly lovely. Called her up from Detroit the day we left for Sacremento, Calif. Sept. 7th. Had a miserable train ride out and spent most of the time in an upper berth. Equipped my brand new B-24 for combat and left for Hamilton Field, San Francisco Sunday night Sept. 13th., my birthday, had dinner at Fisherman's Wharf with Ed Devine, Helen Rothaug, Charlie Herman and Tom Doyle. I had Olympia oysters but never again. My ship springs a leak in the wing tanks so I'm not able to take off with the squadron for Hickam Field Hawaii. Davis takes off on his bomb bay tanks, loses two engines and crashes into San Franscio Bay Sept. 19th 1942. Bill Gunther is lost. Go back to Sacremento to have tanks fixed. Get briefed and ready to leave for Hawaii 29 Sept. but receive orders to go back to Patterson Field, Ohio to pick up some Group property left there in the old ships. Await confirmation of orders until October 1st then strike out dropping Doyle off in Kansas City and Davis in Jackson, Miss. Called Mary Frances from Jackson – She was in school at Hollins, Va. and promised to meet me the next day at the Shoram Hotel in Washington, DC, the only place I could think of to meet her in a three minute conversation. Oct. 3d. I am convinced she is the nicest girl I have ever known. I stayed at the Willard and she stayed with an old school chum. Washington is rather dull but is enhanced by the charming Miss Smith.

Spent Sat. and Sun. at Patterson and arrive back at Sacremento Oct. 5th. Briefed for Hickam on Oct. 9th and leave Hamilton for Hawaii Oct. 10th, 1942 at 4:30 AM. The formation becomes scattered because of thick fog so we agree to brave the broad Pacific alone. Sugden, the "Eastern Yid," navigator, assures me he can do it. I have to fly instruments on account of rain and stratus at all levels up to 10,000 feet for two and a half hours. I'm not ashamed to admit I was a little nervous but blame it on the lack of sleep. Good weather encountered about 800 miles out but two engines try to cut out. Part of my heart is still out there to identify the spot. Arrive Wheeler Field at 4 PM. A glorious reunion with the boys and plenty of bottled delight is produced to substantiate mutual good will. Hardy is believed to be the only casualty.

Honolulu, Waikiki Beach, Scofield and all the rest are somewhat disappointing in their war paint. Practice bombing and search missions help kill rather dull days. Smith, Doyle, Shaffer and I buy an automobile but keep it only 10 days as rumors of our leaving become fact. Feminine contingent of dance held at Wheeler Field Officers Club looks like League of Nations.

Oct. 26, 1942 we leave Wheeler for New Caledonia or Australia in two elements. Spent first night on Christmas Island. The Island is perfectly flat, a couple or three miles wide and not over fifteen miles long, but looks after so much water. The first thing the radio tower wants to know is whether we have mail or not. "Goona, goona" birds that are hardly able to fly, sand crabs and a few coconut trees are the only native flora and fauna. Bunk in a cabin with two pilots returning from search missions for Eddie Rickenbacker. They've had no luck. Three weeks later Rickenbacker is picked up off a rock by a Navy Patrol ship Nov. 15. The man is indestructible.

Oct., 27 we leave Christmas Island for Somoa. Land at Tutuilla Airport occupied by Marines. Doyle and Snyden report seeing a sub just off the Island but Marines discourage them and call it a whale. We spend the night in BOQ just across the bay from "Coconut Head" where the movie "Hurricane" was filmed. The Island is the most beautiful thing I've ever seen since I left Mary Frances. Have to spend the next day there on account of Maj. Faulkner's engine trouble. That night Doyle and I are invited to a feast at the hut of one of the native chiefs. He explains that his wife's father is a "High Talking Chief" and rules many more natives than himself. He gets it over to us in broken English that one of a chief's duty is to defend culprit at a council. The culprit sits in on it with a sack over his head so that he doesn't know who is doing the talking. If the chief can't talk his client out of the trouble the culprit is executed. However, if the tribe doesn't think the chief is a good enough talker they execute him. The best thing about the system is that the chief doesn't think justice is administered, he personally fights it out and the culprit goes happily back to his fish and poi. On the credit side, the chief is given everything his tribe produces and he in turn dishes it out as he sees fit. Shades of the Feudal System!

Oct., 29 we left Samona for Nandi, Fiji landed at 12 noon, a day later Oct 30th since we had passed the international date line. Ate dinner, awed at the native blacks and imported Hindu's and laughed at a big advertisement reading "Fiji – where romance still lives." Took off again at 2:00 PM and flew to Plains de Gaics, New Caledonia some 800 miles from Fiji arriving there in time for the orneriest meal yet, consisting of hunks of half cooked potatoes, something raw resembling spam and powdered milk. It was here that we expected a certain general to order us to stop and make our permanent base. Spirits are low in view of this fact and in view of the dismal looking mountainous island made more awful by the sun setting behind some storm clouds out over that lonesome Pacific. Home never seemed further away and I resolved that if I ever got back I'd build a huge wall around my house to keep any of the atmosphere of New Caledonia from seeping in. We all feel so much

13

better when Maj. Faulkner returns from Headquarters and joyously announces that we must go on to Australia that we don't mind sleeping on the ground under the wing of the ship.

October 31, 1942 we landed on the big continent "down under" at Amberly Field, Ipowitch just 20 miles from Bisbane. After a wonderful meal of fresh, clean cooked eggs and fairly crisp bacon, fresh milk, bread and jam everyone but the maintenance men were allowed to go to town. We took a tram from Ipswitch to Brisbane, 20 miles and 17 stops. The city is about 200,000 population but no buildings over five stories high. Just walking the streets was fun for awhile until we got hungry and began looking for a place to eat. I don't believe thay have over ten restaurants in the whole city. By the time we were finished the city was dimmed out and it didn't look a bit good. Hardly anyone on the streets but servicemen from the U.S. and the Aussies in their knee length shorts. Passed several over-crowded dance halls but could not get more than a peek inide. They do some sort Canadian three step and it is amazing to see everyone of at least five hundred move at exactly the same time. The music is American but but extremely "corny." The English system of money presents its usual difficulties. Arrive back at Amberly Field by tram around one a.m., pretty tired and hungry. A guy with a push cart sold me a pie but it turned out to be some sort of hot, flavorous beef and I threw it away.

Nov., 1st – we arrived at our semi-permanent base at Moreba some 1100 miles north of Brisbane. Now we are really back in the sticks. The 19th Group, whom we are relieving, are very glad to see us and there is free beer at the officers day room. Pitched tent and prepared to call this place home for a while at least. The first two weeks were spent familiarizing ourselves with the war situation as concerned us, swimming in a nice little rocky stream and shooting pistols and rifles. Word comes that we are to leave here and go to Iron range around November 13. The new base is 200 miles north and right on the eastern coast where Australia begins to flatten out on top. The other three squadrons move up but our ships aren't yet in shape for the move. Word comes to us on Nov. 17 that the second mission our Group leaves on, Lt. Larson's ship cuts out on take off causing him to run into two B-24's and a B-17 parked close to the runway. The ship catches on fire and all bombs on board explode killing around 14 men and destroying 4 ships. Werner gets lost returning and lands on a small uncharted island off the coast of New Guinea. Thornhill never reaches the objective and runs out of gas just off shore from Iron Range. No one is hurt in either of these two crews but we are pretty anixous about Eddie Devine who is with Werner somewhere off the coast of New Guinea. This brings the resume up to date and the diary will be kept categorically as near as possible from here on out. Today is Nov. 18, 1942. The 43rd Group sent out four ships at 1:00 AM last night. They are returning now. Have not accertained what results they had. Later – raids on Rabual fairly successful. Lt. Brown of our squadron comes down from Iron Range and reports that Col. Meehan and Maj. Norris are also missing from the raid day before yesterday. That makes seven B-24's more or less washed up since we started operating one week ago – one a day – Tomorrow we leave here for Iron Range as our ships are ready to ride.

Thursday Oct., 19 – Sunday October 22. Spent the last four days making our new camp a semblance of home. Had time to read "A London Diary" by Quentin Reynolds and a "Thousand Shall Fall" by Hans Habe. The first took me two hours and the second took me two days. The first told how England was saved from Hitler by the RAF and the second told how France was betrayed. Doyle, Shaffer and I took a trek into the jungle yesterday. It's as full of wonders as I always thought it would be. There are many wild boar, crocodiles and pythons all around us but to reconcile that fact I have seen some of the most beautiful birds in the world. Their whistles and calls make the place a little more livable. One enlisted man caught and tamed a bird that looks like a pigeon but for its brilliant plumage. Every tent should have one – they make a wonderful afternoon's entertainment.

This morning (Sunday) there were no Protestant services as our chaplain is with the ground echelon still on the way across the Pacific. Heaven knows I wish they'd hurry and arrive. Every inconvenience that we now contend with is expected to disappear when the ground echelon gets here. I haven't had a letter since I left Oahu.

Tonight George Shaffer just came puffing in with the news that we were going out on our first mission right away. There's much excitement and speculation. I'd better get going.

Monday morning – We took off last night at 1:30 and got back about 9:30. A very disappointing trip as far as I was concerned. We reached the target, Lae Airdrome, in good shape but spent an hour and a half there trying to open the bomb bay doors. There was very little flak – the weather wasn't too bad. The other boys had quite a few duds in their bombs but San Francisco radio says today that we destroyed nineteen Zero's and put some holes in their runway. My compass was over 20 degrees off and we got ourselves lost coming back. Landed with about an hour's fuel aboard. Slept most all day. Tonight we are going to get around some Sparkling Hoch – something like champagne. Tuesday Nov 24th. Last nights party was a success. Higgins was the winner, I guess, with "The Eyes of Texas Are Upon You," and "the illogic of changing the name of Arkansas to Arkanas." Sleep came easy for me most all day. I did take time out to build a platform for my cot to sit upon. Makes it higher and the blankets don't drag in the sand floor. Everyday we kill four or five sand spiders and centipedes.

Wednesday we left here for Townsville to pick up some of our ground echelon who have just arrived by boat. They all got loaded in the planes next day – Thanksgiving – and some colonel came out, made them unload and ordered us to take some Ordnance men to Port Moresby. Got there just before dark Thanksgiving Day. Hottest damn place I've ever seen. Tried to sleep under a blanket to keep off the mosquitoes, no luck. Finally dropped off about 12 but was awakened by an air raid. Your first raid is something you'll always remember! Three ships were focused directly in the lights but couldn't be brought down although I know they were hit by fragments. I couldn't get into a foxhole so I stood there in my underwear watching them and was literally eaten up by mosquitoes. There were about seven or eight planes in the raid. Got back in bed at three thirty. The all clear sounded and we piled back out of bed not knowing what signal it was. In the midst of the bombing I had some enlisted man over on another hilltop calling for Dr. Kildare. If those boys didn't have a sense of humor they would have less than nothing. The bombers look like they're heading directly for you and you alone. They never hit anything of importance.

Friday I left Mosesby for Iron Range after being towed out of the mud holes. Just heard, but refuse to believe that only two of Werner's crew got out alive. They say Eddie Devine is buried on the beach near Bouganville Island. It just can't be. Seems like he ought to bringing us a watermelon or a keg of beer or something right now. I'm not going to say anything about Eddie. There's too much to say because there was so much to him. He was all heart and MY boy.

Sat. – So far today I've been up and practiced gunnery dropped 20 practice bombs and swung my compass. It's now twelve o'clock and time for lunch without water. There's a rumor that we will to leave the "Range" shortly as the rainy season is about here. There's supposed to be 200 inches in the next two months. Runways and revetments would be useless to try to keep up. I wonder where the "Gypsy 90th" will go to next. I may go on another mission this afternoon. I think the target will be an old derelict off shore from Buna. A B-25 dropped down to look it over yesterday and got shot down. They are pretty sure the Japs have been using it as a submarine base and all sorts of listening devices are aboard as well as heavy anti-aircraft guns. Well, it's too bad for the yellow boys if they send me out today after that practice this morning. Doyle can pick out which side of their hair he wants to part.

Sunday was a day of rest. I finished *Kitty Foyle* by Christopher Morley. There was a victim of circumstances that I feel sorry for. Doyle disagrees and says it just reflects on the Orange Irish because she married a Jew. Mother says she has some sort of package on the way for Christmas. I feel a little remorseful of that because I'm absolutely unable to reciporcate. Something for Mary Frances is a problem too. What can I possibly do for them without even a telegraph office near here. If only they will start the "leave system" in time for me to go to Sydney before Dec. 25th. Someday maybe they'll be able to read this and know I'm at least thinking about them. HOW I'm thinking about them!

The Tokyo radio is a scream. Last night they mentioned that they hadn't forgotten about us at Iron Range. Advised that we were about to move out, they were very uncomplimentary to the boys in the 30th Squadron who bombed their Geisha Girl houses up at Rabaul the other night. After their fantistic news report they always play "Home Sweet Home" sung in Japanese and let some prisoners of war speak to their folks back home. They all have to say they torpedoed by an Allied sub and were picked up by a Japanese vessel. That girl that sings "Home Sweet Home" sounds like an amateur playing a saw. It's very pathetic and I know Steven Foster would object. I object myself.

December 9th Wednesday. A helluva lot has taken place since I last wrote this diary up. Knew when I began that I couldn't keep it up daily. Anyway, last Wednesday all four squadrons went out to attack some Jap destroyers on the west coast of Guinea near Buna. Apparently they were coming down from Rabaul. The 319th hit them first but were intercepted by Zero's – about 30 of them according to Col. Rogers. That was around five forty five PM. The 400th found them next at 6:30 and got some near misses. We got there in time to see the last bombs of the 400th. All close but no hits. Major Faulkner was leading the first element and I was leading the second. We were to drop on his bombs but he had rack trouble causing us to make several dry runs. Doyle and I got disgusted and decided to do our own syncronizing and let go with 4 500 -pound bombs. Two hit short and two smacked the tail end of a destroyer. It was getting too dark to do any further bombing so we headed for home pretty happy at any rate. Don't know whether they were going into Buna for evacuation or replacements. However, their plans were frustrated even though it hasn't been established that the ship was sunk. The 319th got four Zero's in the foray but were shot up considerably.

Sunday my ship and crew were to go out to Rabaul. The weather was stinking and the plans not well coordinated. We didn't get off. The 3 ships that did were unable to find the target.

Monday night our squadron went out to bomb the runways at Gasmata. More weather and no moon. Major Faulkner led the first element and I led the second. We flew D.R. up there and dropped one bomb at a time along what we thought was the coast hoping they would open up on us with ack-ack and search lights. They never opened and we came back alone as the formation was unable to stick together in such bad weather. Our own search lights were up when we got back. That saved us. We'd never found our own field without them.

Yesterday Squadron went out without me. They were to pick up a target and get briefed at Port Moresby. They have just begun to come back in right now. It's getting dark again. My ship and crew are on alert – assigned to the 320th. We may go out tonight. I'm getting sick of this business. Captain Taylor was transferred to the 320th as C.O. about a week ago. I got my old job back as Operations Officer, thus making me second in command of the squadron. Lots of headaches and responsibility but I believe I can do it as well or better than anyone else so that's justification I suppose.

The rains have started and are rather unpleasant. Everything in the tent gets sopping including the bed clothes. War is hell and a wet bed doesn't help ease the pain.

Sunday December 13th. Since my last experiment with laundering in which all my clothes were tinted baby blue, I've been racking my brain for some solution. There's a chink in the squadron who wants to be a gunner. Today I think I changed his mind. I gave him permission to pick any helper he wanted and to name his price for laundry work. He had my half ton all day and is getting a big kick out of it. I believe he's forgotten all about shooting a "Yap."

In my spare time I've become quite a craftsman. I've made several rings out of Australian copus. Took a florin and hammered the edges out flat then then bored the middle out to fit my finger. A shilling thus beaten on makes a nice girls' ring. Rather a nice ring for a girl. This afternoon I made two fly swatters, a very handy article, out of an old inner tube and some screen wire.

I forgot to mention that on a raid off Buna in which I participated Norman Crossman and his crew lost the formation and failed to return. Our first ship and crew lost in combat. Just realized that myself and Crawford, Shaffer and Higgins are the only four officers of the original 321st Bomber Squadron.

December 23rd. Wednesday – The Good Lord is with me I know. For ten days (since I last wrote) we have been chasing a Japanese convoy all over the South Pacific. We caught two cruisers and two destroyers up near Gasmata, were intercepted by Zero's and had a sky full of flak to bomb in. The Zero's came in from everywhere and their acrobatics are a sight to behold. A couple of them will get just out of range and put on an aerial show. You can't afford to get fascinated because at the same time another couple are sneaking in from another angle. It's a good trick nevertheless and the Zero is credited with being the most maneuverable fighters in the world. I doubt it not. What our B-24's is a little fighter escort as I hear they're getting them in the Aleutians. We spent the night at Moresby. Next day, intelligence reports showed a convoy from Rabual heading for NaDang composed of four destroyers, two cruisers and two transports. The transports were our objectives. The 400th hit them first and were shot up pretty much. The 319th was next and we were intercepted. Lost a tail gunner and two waist gunners.

We found them in the Vittles Straights just before dark. Broke formation and went in on them individually. Shaffer dropped a stick of four 500 pound bombs on a cruiser and it went to the bottom at 10 that night. Spent the next night in ME and went back out after the convoy who by now had decided to go back to the Admiralty Islands. Passed the shadow ship on the way up. It was Captain Jones. He'd been intercepted and had three men wounded including the co-pilot. The 319th had just left and Captain Patterson's ship went down somewhere on Guinea. We found the target and got two hits on a cruiser. Don't think it was sunk though. The 320th lost a ship, Lt. Adams, on the way up there in the bad weather. Severe icing was the cause. The same day another shadows ship, Lt. Rafferty failed to return, cause unknown. We left Moresby December 20th for Iron Range. Never thought I'd be glad to see this place but it sure looked good.

Intelligence just reported that word had come from Lt. Cresson who was believed lost. He crash landed his ship near Burke, Australia

Dec 3rd. Four crew members had stayed with the ship and six jumped. Two that stayed were killed and there is a search out for the six that jumped. We sent three planes to search for them. Wildest damn country I ever saw. Plenty of water buffalo, wild cattle and wild horses. We returned without locating the wreck or the chutes. Cresson has sent a couple more wires that he's apparently out of the hospital. He's going to go from from Burkestown to Cloncerry, the nearest airport and we'll pick him up there when he arrives. It's about 200 miles but it will take him at least two weeks to make it. No roads at all. Northern Australia is very primitive and the Aborigines are so black they're almost blue. The most surprising thing in the world is to hear one of them open his mouth and speak with an almost Eaton accent. The one's with the bushy hair, incidentally were originally head hunters but are now quite friendly. Nevertheless I have so far avoided the bushy headed type.

Today is Christmas Eve and I've just been told by the dentist, Joe Black, that I have a wisdom tooth that is frightening. Don't know why he should be frightened. To compensate for this bad news some mail has just come in. Two letters from Mother and one from Mary Frances, all dated Oct 28th. Mary Frances also sent me a leather cigarette case that matches the billfold she sent me in Hawaii. That's my sweetie! Wish I had a picture of her – a big one. Mother's letters were newsy and encouraging. I seem to want to choke up on them a little though.

Christmas Day I left for Port Moresby to fight the war for a week. Went on three reconnaissance missions of 9 hours duration each. One day we bombed a warehouse at Madang and another at Finchaven. They're more nerve wracking than the mosquitoes we fight all night. Got back to Iron Range on the 30th and have just been reminiscing last New Year's in San Antonio with Gordon Benedict and Peg Robson or rather Gordon and Peg Benedict they had just become. Yesterday afternoon we went out to the jetties and watched them unload two cargo ships. Pulled our rank and got a ride around the bay in a neat little cabin cruiser job that belonged to Paramount before the war. Went swimming later and came back with a whale of an appetite. Crosson had been flown in the meantime and I had a long talk with him. He was lost 13 days during which time he had two muscles, some grass and some dysentery medicine for food. He and his radio operator wandered around the first two days without knowing each others name and thinking there were three of them along. They swam rivers the natives would not even get near because of sharks and crocodiles. At night they covered themselves with mud to keep off the mosquitoes. They traveled through country that the blacks say has never been traveled by a white man. After 13 days of it, one morning they dropped off to sleep and were awakened by some shouting. It was a white man and an Aborigine. They started yelling their heads off and scared the two men on horses. They went the other way, thinking Crosson might be Japanese. When they finally saw they weren't armed they picked them up and led them to the ranch. Crosson had to cut his socks off. He went from 205 pounds down to 155 in those 13 days.

Today is January 12, 1943. Tuesday. I went back to Moresby on the 3d and returned Sat night Jan. 9th. Tomorrow I think I'll be going back up. While I was there the last time we pulled a daylight raid on Rabual. You never saw so many ships in one harbor. The Zeke's weren't too active but the ack ack was intense. We all understand now why they weren't active. The next day the recco ship sighted a convoy of five transports four destroyers and two cruisers. They went into Lea under constant bombardment from the Air force. Two transports and maybe three were definitely sunk. 68 Zero's were shot down or damaged. Lt. Altman failed to return as well as Higgings and Rose. Higgins had sent in a report of his approximate position just before he crashed so I got busy on it and searched the area north of Goodenough Island. It was the greatest mission I've ever been on – we found them on Islet Island. Eight of the ten survived. We dropped them water, food, blankets and mosquito nets then went back to Melne Bay and got the Catalina out there in a hurry. It was a magnificent feeling to save someone's life and it makes a lot more sense than the work I'm doing most of the time.

Shaffer and I went over to the 319th area last night to visit the boys. Muscatel wine sure makes you sing. An Aussie taught us a song called "Waltzing Matilda." Everybody is singing it today. It sure looked bad though last night in their club to see those new faces. They realize it as much as we do that they're replacements for some of the best guys I've ever known. Please Lord don't make it necessary to put anyone in my place. I've thought a lot about reincarnation lately. It seems so useless to live just the short while I've lived. There are so many things to live for when you sit down and count them. But if I should go, I'd like to think I have another chance to come back and live life in its entirety.

NOTE: Lieutenant McMurria and his crew were shot down January 20, 1943. Their ordeal for the next two and one-half years follows in a great epic story of survival at the brutal hands of the Japanese military.

While I was there the last time we pulled a daylight raid on Rabaul. You never saw so many ships in one harbor. The Zekes weren't too active but the ack ack was intense. We all understand now why they weren't active. The next day the recco ship sighted a convoy of 5 transports 4 destroyers and two cruisers. The went into Lea under constant bombardment from the air force. Two transports and maybe three were definately sunk. 68 zeros were shot down or damaged. Lt. Altman failed to return as well as Higgins and Rose. Higgins had sent in a report of his approximate position just before he crashed so we got busy on it and searched the area north of Goodenough Island. It was the greatest mission I've ever been on - We found them.

**Actual Diary Page**

My good friend Smitty wrote this letter to my mother in Columbus, Georgia for which I am eternally grateful. He returned home safely and now lives in Newport Beach, California. When he wrote this letter, however, it included all the information he or anyone else knew of my whereabouts - the following pages relate to what happened.

*January 23, 1943*
*Somewhere in the South Pacific*

*Dear Mrs. McMurria,*

*.I hope this diary your son kept will some day reach you. I'll
enter all the information I know in this note to you and leave
instructions to have it mailed to you after the war. I happen to know
that it contains impressions and thoughts of your son, though it is
not for me to read, and I am sure he would want it to reach you.
Since he was one of the very best friends I ever had and I feel that
I was very close to him, I am taking the liberty of writing to tell
you what happened and pray that he will soon come back to be able
to tell us his adventures.*

*First of all, let me say that "Mac" and I mutually agreed to
write each other's families and girls should anything happen. It
seemed much better to send a human message than the cold, crisp
"Missing in Action" notice the Army sends out. Therefore, please
relate the following story to Mary Frances Smith, who lives in
Greenville, S.C., and during the school terms attends Hollins
College, Virginia.*

*What I am going to say would not be passed by the censors, so
I will see that this is mailed to you after all that is past history.*

*On January 14 our squadron flew to Port Moresby to take over
bombing and reconnaissance duties for a week. January 15 Mac and
his crew went out on a Recco (reconnaissance) and ran into six Zeros
on their way home. They shot down three. Tom Doyle, bombardier
from Kansas City, Kansas, got one and two other crew members got
the other two. The tail gunner was shot in the leg, breaking it, and
all returned safely.*

*On January 16 six ships took off for a night raid on Rabaul.
Three ships turned back because of nasty weather, but your son was
one of those to go on through and bomb the place.*

*January 20 was the day Mac did not return and I'm man enough
to say that I couldn't keep tears from filling my eyes, for he was*

*more a brother than a friend. Fellows become awfully close over here and carrying on the work we're doing. Mac and his crew were on a Recco up the northwest coast of New Guinea. The trip went up as far as Wewak. They were to cut out over the ocean covering the northern shipping lanes and return to Port Moresby. Mac sent in a report that he had seen 22 Zeros on the airfield at Wewak. Three minutes later he sent in another report that he had sighted a convoy of two transports and three destroyers off Wewak and that three Zeros were attacking him. That is the last message we ever had from him.*

*Five ships took off for Wewak to bomb the convoy after receiving his message and when they arrived the convoy could not be found, but 22 to 25 Zeros attacked the formation and shot the ships up badly, though miraculously no one was injured, and 12 Zeros were shot down in a running battle of 45 minutes.*

*January 21, George Shaffer and I, the other half of our tent, went out on a search for Mac, Tom, and crew. We thoroughly searched every island from Finshafen to Wewak and were convinced that no trace of Mac or any parts of their plane had landed or washed up on these islands. This was hopeful in a way as no sign is a good sign. This left two conclusions, one hopeful and one fateful. Either they tried to shake the Zeros by going on out to sea, and if so all is lost, or they circles back to be over land, in which case they'll get back in a month or two. We are praying for the latter and, knowing Mac as we do, believe that he did circle back over land.*

*In closing let me say that it has been one of the luckiest and greatest pleasures of my life to have known and associated with your son and Tom Doyle. It seems impossible for God to prohibit the return of such decent, clean, brave, upstanding fellows as these and every night we'll keep on praying for their return.*

*Very sincerely yours,*

*Haviland Smith*
*1045 Chaffee Place*
*Daytona Beach, Florida*

Convoy Attack Mission – Japanese Naval Convoy
Rabaul, New Britain

# PREFACE

The enormity of World War II is confusing even to those whose lives were touched by it, and, understandably, it will become even more so to future generations as fantasies and facts entwine with political and personal bias clouding the minds of those who regard the epic from the distant 21st century.

On August 31, 1939, Adolph Hitler, for his own reasons and needing an excuse to light the fuse to Europe, sent seven German soldiers disguised in Polish uniforms to the Polish border town of Gleiwitz. The faking of an invasion of Germany by these soldiers marks this border incident as the fountainhead of what was to come. Hitler's Panzers rolled and the world was on fire for six years thereafter.

Serious students will debate the issues interminably. The layman will go on believing what he cares to believe with little effort to unravel the Gordian knot. Sad to say, I am a layman.

The discipline required of me to write Trial and Triumph stemmed largely from my belief that many will, as human nature dictates, interest themselves in specific drama of the war rather than the fundamental causes or cataclysmic results.

Another strong reason for my efforts herewith was the discovery in our attic of letters written by relatives during the War Between the States. To me, they are equally as interesting and certainly less fatiguing than deciphering the guilt or innocence of Jefferson Davis or the wisdom of Abraham Lincoln.

I hope my descendants and perhaps others will find that what I have written adds flavor to their knowledge of certain aspects of the war in the Pacific and something of how it was conducted. This is not a hero's story; it is simply a soldier's story of "Trial and Triumph."

James Austin McMurria
Greenville, South Carolina
April, 1991

Bomb run on a Japanese war ship.

# Chapter 1

The little bell inside the field telephone rang so softly it would hardly wake you up at night, because it lay in its small brown leather case on top of dirty laundry and khaki uniforms that absorbed most of its sound. In the daytime it seldom rang, and there was seldom anyone there to answer it if it did.

I remember the day the enlisted men strung the wire up the hill to our tent and installed it. I felt it gave me, the squadron operations officer, a certain amount of prestige since only the C.O. and myself shared such a status symbol in our camp. It was connected, of course, to various offices like the supply tent, the adjutants office and the mess tent. With a little patience you could even talk to the other three squadrons of the 90th Bomb Group encamped on the other side of the runway several miles away.

The fast pace the New Guinea war had been taking for the last 30 days in '42, however, had now reduced this thing of convenience to an object of hate. I seldom had the opportunity or the inclination to use it frivolously anymore. Too many neighbors were missing and even the Christmas mail plane we'd all counted on so heavily had gotten lost on the flight up from Brisbane. So there was little news to spread around and a lot less to joke about over the private telephone. And yet I couldn't hate the thing completely, because just a few days before it had provided me an unusual diversion.

Neither Doyle, Shaffer nor Smitty were around at the time and I found myself alone in our tent. It was a lonely tent and a lonely northern Australia. A lonely war like most wars. To escape its depression I lapsed temporarily into a world of make believe and picked up the phone's heavy receiver. Without thumbing the transmitting switch or turning the crank that signaled the other receivers, I half thought, half mumbled enthusiastic conversations to several friends and my parents back in the states. The self deception had been good for me until a small scorpion crawling on the sand floor of our tent brought me back to reality. The effort of killing the scorpion and the approaching Oklahoma drawl of George Shaffer coming up the hill through the giant ironwood trees promptly relocated me at Iron Range, Cape York Peninsular,

Queensland longitude 143 degrees East, latitude 12 degrees South. The guilt of my childish fantasy must have given Shaffer an idea of what I'd been doing because at that very moment the phone rang and I was completely disorganized. As I fumbled for the leather case to answer it Shaffer said ironically and without knowing the context "If it's from Tulsa, I'm here."

It wasn't Oklahoma and it wasn't Georgia but the undisguised buoyancy the C.O.'s voice, that hadn't been so buoyant lately, gave me a suspicion that something pleasant might be in the air for a change. Under the circumstances it wasn't too hard for me to break off abruptly from the phone and continue the conversation in his tent three minutes later. Three minutes isn't very long to speculate but when wishful thinking grips you right down to the soles of your G.I. shoes there's plenty of time to work things out the way you want it. It wasn't the first time the idea of a fortuitous truce between us and the Japanese had entered my mind. It had entered a lot of our not so courageous minds if we would admit it. Replacement?...that was out too, we hadn't been in the thick of it long enough. Reinforcement might be good enough for the time being. An additional bomb group stationed here wouldn't cure the short tempers, the grips, the alibis, the occasional aborted mission that really shouldn't have aborted but it would sure help. Unconsciously my mind was fixed on these happy thoughts as I lifted the mosquito netting that protected the entrance to Maj. Faulkner's canvas sleeping quarters. There was little formality in a tee shirt and a 5 o'clock shadow.

"You didn't have to run," he told me. "The news isn't that good." I partially collapsed on the vacant cot feeling a little let down by his first remark but ready to come to life if the situation warranted it.

"We're going back to Port Moresby for four more days," Faulkner said. The way he let the word "days" drop I knew he wasn't through. I withheld my oath of disgust. "I know we just got back and I know we're short of crews but we're going. I didn't argue with Group. But you and I are going to make a little policy here and now that might shake the whole 5th Air Force but by God we're gonna make it." I was now sitting upright on the edge of the cot nodding agreement to any act of defiance he was prepared to propose. Cecil Faulkner was an old timer, having been at Pearl Harbor when it was hit on the morning of infamy and was in the regular Air Force. On top of that he was an outstanding pilot and regular in a lot more ways. It was easy to let him lead and if he was ready to defy or in any way reshuffle the back breaking routine we were under, he was still the leader and he could count on me.

His proposal was completely realistic and again demonstrated the kind of man he was. There couldn't be any replacements at this time and he knew it. There weren't any available groups in the states to reinforce us and he knew that too. An unsuspected truce or an end to the war was sophomoric. He probably never indulged himself along the lines that I had just done, even when nobody was looking. The sweat at Pearl and at Midway had dehydrated the romance of a young war and molded a serial number with experience and ability to command. His proposal made sense.

The War Dept. was a lot further away in 1942 than the 11,000 miles that separated us on the map. The early confusion created by a humiliating defeat, an inadequate striking force and the pressure of policy and politics was in the bloodstream and the wounded heart was pumping the infection out to the corporal extremities. Cecil Faulkner knew a little first aid and here on the side of a hill at Iron Range he was about to administer it. Rotating a crew every 10 days for rest and recuperation in Sidney was the antidote and just the idea was immediately efficacious. We shouldn't even get any bitching from Group on this one. Even old Col. Rogers looked tired these days.

A part of my exuberance for the plan in all honesty, couldn't help but have come from the intimate knowledge I had of the serial numbers in my squadron. Somebody had to go first and I wouldn't be far behind. Again Faulkner's maturity evolved and it was decided that the equitable basis for rotation to bars and belles in Sydney should be based on the number of combat missions each crew had flown rather than on seniority. A quick mental calculation on my part put me in full agreement, although I don't believe the major had the slightest idea that he and I were tied for first crack at the trip.

There was no town, no village, no farmers, or ranchers that I ever saw living around Iron Range, Australia. There were some crude docking facilities in its sheltered harbor a few miles from the air strip, but I never saw anyone tending it. Occasionally an ancient Australian barge of some dreary type would pull in there and a handful of Aussies would appear from the jungle and swap yarns with the crew until it moved quietly on. The forbidding rain forest circumscribed every man made scar on the area it had dominated for millions of years. Undoubtedly the name of the place was given it by some lonely geologist who first scratched its surface and found iron ore. Perhaps an assault had been made upon its hills to excavate the stuff but the advancing green growth had long since disguised the futile effort and the evidence was hidden. Situated as it is on the narrow finger of land at the northeast extremity of Australia called the Cape York Peninsular, it receives maritime tropical breezes from the Gulf of Carpenteria on its left and the Torres Straits on its right. It is supposed to receive 200 inches of rain in 60 days during the wettest season. There is no dry season. It could get chilly at night and I believe as dark as any place on earth with a little help from an overcast to hide it sometimes brilliant equatorial sky. In the low areas dividing the hills were black shallow pools of stagnant water. Huge trees often stood in the middle of these pools much like our cypress, but their roots or knees were sometimes five feet above the water and extended themselves 10 or 12 feet toward the drier floor of the forest. Once on a short trek into the jungle for relaxation I saw a living object slither from the mud around one of these pools into the shallow water. Someone shot it with a .45 caliber pistol and fished it out with a long bamboo pole. It was a horrible looking fish like the one whose picture you see in the dictionary with an unpronounce-able name, not quite evolved from its prehistoric state. No one touched it with his bare hand. No one cared to handle the parrots we occasionally shot. The wallabies we shot had the saddest eyes of all the lonesome creatures in this lonely land, except for the eyes of the combat crews of the 321st Squadron.

Now fortified with a strong counter balance, I hurried back up the hill to alert the crews with the bad news first. "Prepare to leave in the morning for five more days at Moresby and at least four more missions," I announced rather casually. Shipping was still the prime target and each mission could be counted on for a minimum of eight or nine hours; thirty to forty hours of anxiety over Jap waters along, and with green navigators against combat seasoned Japanese pilots flying the most maneuverable fighters in any theatre--the Zero.

"If you'll quit ya bitchin and sit back down, I might make you bellyachers smile for a change." I shouted, directing my remark at Higgins, who frequently had such proclivities after having already been shot down once. Gestures of the hands and open mouths were simultaneously frozen and immobilized. "Now what," was the collective and yet unuttered question.

"Every mother's son of you with anything that qualifies as a combat mission is gonna get 10 days in Sidney, one crew at a time beginning as soon as this five night stand is over. The workers go first and the drones come later. How many missions you got, Crawford?" I tried to walk away while it was quiet, but I heard a bottle of Old Corio bourbon pop and changed my mind. "That makes the cheese more binding," someone said. Nobody discussed the coming five days in Port Moresby anymore that night. We were repainting Sidney Australia in our minds eye.

**Mission Briefing**

Jolly Rogers – Mission – Target Rabaul

# Chapter 2

By the time a B-24 has grudgingly submitted to the will of its pilot and agreed to become airborne against its own iron will, the human ego is once again satisfied in the knowledge that brain is bigger than brawn. Several tons of dead weight that has been furiously resisting gravity down a magnetic runway slowly acknowledges the end of its earth bound existence and is reincarnated into something a bit more graceful than the Wright Brothers first plane but not a lot more, according to us. We had bought the idea that a B-24 could carry a bigger bomb load and that it could carry it further than a B-17, but she was still one helluva sight getting off the ground and doing it. We wondered if she could take punishment and then she just plain wasn't slick like the old Boeing on which most of us had cut our teeth. "Just something else to bitch about," had been Faulkner's comment. Actually, we were the first group of Americans in combat in the Pacific with the new Consolidate B-24's, and there was a lot to be proven. Well, the next five days would in all probability give the statisticians a lot more basis for comparison of the two planes.

Once off the air strip and pointed toward Port Moresby, New Guinea, you know immediately why the area is called the Great Barrier Reef. Knife-like hulks of coral with a foamy yellow collar emerge from the shallow green ocean in every direction. You feel that when this continent was born a few more labor pains from the mother volcano would have made it fifty miles wider all the way down its eastern coast for five hundred miles. The coral took many unusual shapes both above and below the water but especially under it where it was more massive. On a dull practice mission these underwater forms sometimes fascinated you like clouds as the perspective changed while you moved along from a good altitude and with oblique sunlight. It even worked with moonlight but the features where less sharp. Looking down through a thin, scattered undercast the patterns became even more checkered as clouds blended with coral and became indistinguishable.

The cloud cover that usually forms over water at night was being burnt off by the morning sun and was dissipating slowly below the 321st Squadron as we jockeyed and trimmed ourselves into a loose formation that would deploy us at the staging area facing the Japanese.

Arriving at Moresby after an hour's flight, I noticed that nothing had changed about Jackson Airdrome in a week that I could see except that there were a dozen or so C-47's parked along the steel mesh runway that I hadn't seen there before. Evidently a transport group had just arrived giving the airdrome commander insufficient time to build horseshoe revetments with his bulldozers in which to park the new arrivals. I was sure the transport pilots would be unhappy about that tonight when and if the Japs came over. In spite of their so-called primitive Japanese bomb sight, we were still losing planes on the ground and I never saw anyone stay out of a slit trench when it was available if the Nips looked serious at all. But that was their worry and my problem was to get down and find my own revetment. The "follow me" jeeps made that easy for us and sure enough we were again taking that dangerous jeep ride over pot holes and mud at full throttle toward the operation shack. The only bunch of guys that seemed happier than base personnel who took combat crews to operations for their mission orders, were the armament crews that met you when you were lucky enough to come back from a mission, tired and shaken and tried to see how fast they could reload you with bombs and ammo for another mission. It was an enthusiasm we didn't have to accept and certainly no ground crewman smiling all over himself was going to make us like it.

The black board in the line operations shack was like those in a bookie joint: the track, the rider, the horse and the race; the crew, the plane, the target and the time; and here our intelligence really worked. The crew always matched the plane. They even used the plane's name instead of its number. Lt. Crosson was always opposite "Little Eva," and Shaffer was correctly assigned to "Ain't Ya Sorry," their own individual planes. How could they be so accurate in this when at times it seemed certain squadrons were completely overworked and others weren't pulling their load?

The physical condition of various planes was kept on another blackboard. Here the number rather than the same of the plane was used as this board was evidently maintained by the more serious engineering dept. The combat crews resented them least of all as they were inclined to stay out of the way and mind their own business. We came to think of them as our friends and on a rather high intellectual plane until once Hav Smith noticed on their board under REMARKS "Nose wheel broke off." A cynical streak in Smitty prompted the addition of an apostrophe and the letter "N" to the word "off" thus chastening the slide rule department humorously. These blackboards and the men working here were all too familiar to me as I quickly scanned the room in search of my own orders. There was nothing set up for my crew yet, which meant we probably wouldn't go out on a combat mission until tonight.

"How about a little transportation," I asked a rather sleepy looking corporal. "No dice, sir," he replied, "the 43rd Group has all the jeeps tied up. But I can let Private Thurmond here take your crew to the Hotel De Gink in a carry all." De Gink was row of tents accommodating visiting air crews.

"Beats the hell out of walking," said Sgt. Engel, who had already picked up his val pak and didn't want to waste any time getting settled since it interfered with his chances of picking up a poker game with some of his favorite pigeons that were stuck here in Moresby permanently and had lots of chips to gamble.

Port Moresby was the last bastion of defense on New Guinea, except for a small portion of the south coast consisting mostly of native villages and terminating at the extreme S. E. tip with a small garrison and airstrip called Milne Bay. Milne Bay and its fortuitously reinforced Aussie troops had, within the past 90 days, successfully thwarted a strong Japanese invasion force. Moresby was at the moment the supreme objective of the enemy which was now advancing on foot from the north side of New Guinea directly over the Own Stanley Mountains toward Port Moresby, the flood gate into Australia itself.

Being stationed in the very N. E. tip of Australia at Iron Range, our Bomb Group could in a matter of 60 minutes or less, leave the security of an Australian base, refuel our planes at Moresby and reconnoiter and bomb the enemy from this forward base. The Japs

held everything beyond the mountains northward through the
Philippines, Okinawa and Japan itself, some 1800 miles. It was hit
and run for us at the time--Moresby was secure
but severely threatened.

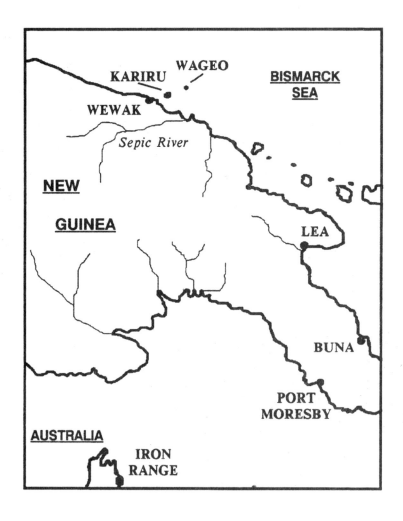

**My Crew**

**James McMurria**

**"Jolly Roger" B-24 Liberator**

In 1942, Port Moresby was the capital of New Guinea and was also the gateway to a world still largely unknown, the forgotten world of the bushmen, who have lived in isolation for a very long time. The enormous distances of this second largest island in the world, its great mountain barriers, its vast tropical rain forests and coastal swamps and savannas prevented communication and travel by its several hundred thousand Melanesians who lived in conditions similar to those of prehistoric man.

As Air Force personnel we could see from above what ground troops of both sides would encounter if fighting developed in the dense jungles, the enveloping swamp lands, the water logged beaches or the burning sun on open grass plains. From the relative safety of our aircraft we could see a panorama of millions of acres of steam beds, bare rocks and undisturbed jungle, sunless and damp under an unbroken leafy canopy unquestionably housing clouds of malaria bearing mosquitoes and vermin of every sort. No adventurous spirit to investigate that awesome wilderness first hand was ever entertained by the air crews. The sight of it from ten thousand feet above was enough for us.

Remembering Faulkner's promise of R & R in Sydney we were eager to take more than our normal ration of combat missions during our four day stint at the forward base. Everyone felt that same compulsion because of the reward it offered.

The box score on January 19th, 1943 was McMurria-19 missions--Faulkner 19--Alfonse and Gaston. Who gets the first leave to Sydney? How could I be so presumptuous as to preempt my own Squadron Commander and take first leave even though Faulkner insisted that I do so.

One more mission would put me clearly ahead in the race and I need not apologize for accepting the reward that could be mine without argument. So for my crew it's off to the northwest Japanese shipping lanes covering Finshafen, Wewak, the Admiralty Island, back down New Britain's coast, through the Vitiaz Straits over the mountains and home to Moresby in about 10 hours. If, if, if and all goes well--look out Sydney here comes a ravenous crew.

At 4 a.m. January 20, 1943, the makeshift weather station at Moresby reported severe thunder storms over the pass through the mountains which was the normal route we flew to the Jap held north coast. We were getting a pretty good rain here at Jackson's Drome at the moment and it looked like a long delay. In my eagerness to get going and get it over with, I proposed to the weather officer that instead of flying a few miles south and trying to get through the pass, why not take off and fly up the south side of New Guinea and cross the mountains after daybreak when conditions would undoubtedly improve and the weather would be less hazardous.

The sleepy weather officer without protest agreed to my suggestion, okayed the flight plan methodically and went back to his canvas cot relieved of the annoyance of our intrusion.

Burnett gave me the signal that the wheel chocks were out and I gingerly pressed the throttle quadrant forward. Four Pratt and Whitney 1200 H.P. engines responded to the touch. Half way down the strip that was lit by a row of smudge pots, the wing lights exposed a threatening accumulation of rain washed sand, mud and gravel on the runway, which seriously cut our airspeed and veered us violently to the side of the runway. Martindale and I immediately realized we couldn't get airborne because of this and simultaneously cut the throttle and stood upright on the brakes. Fifty yards beyond the end of the steel mesh runway we brought the panting bomber to a halt with its nose encased in the barbed wire fence marking the end of the cleared area around the field. A most unceremonious beginning of a flight that was to win us two weeks leave.

I carefully taxied the plane back out of the rough terrain grown up in tall kunai grass and onto the crude runway. Half way back to the other end I idled the engines, got out and inspected the debris that had aborted our take off. Most of it was on the right side so I determined that by hugging the left side on my next attempt I could get the bugger off the ground.

Night take off without runway lights were known to be rather hazardous, even without a load of bombs aboard. There had been

several accidents resulting from this in the past 30 days and one
ship attempting such a takeoff, had dipped its wing into a B-17
parked on the side of the strip blowing both of them to high heaven.

A frantic airdrome officer wildly waving a flashlight careened
his jeep up to my idling engines at the head of the runway and
called for a conference. He insisted that we delay the flight until
the debris was removed. Gung-ho McMurria out talked him in an
effort to get going with visions of Sydney dancing in his head. He
ultimately condescended to let me try again and obliged me by
driving his jeep down to the crap on the runway and illuminating
it with his headlights.

With full flaps and maximum mercury, I unleashed the brakes
of the shuttering plane, skirted down the left side and with great
relief of tension became airborne in the murky night drizzle,
heading up the south coast of New Guinea praying for daylight and
a clear passage over the towering Owen-Stanley mountains on my
right.

Low Pass – Jap merchant ship on fire.

# Chapter 3

It takes about 20 thousand feet to get over the Owen-Stanley Mountains safely, up in the northern part of New Guinea, behind the Japanese stronghold of Wewak. I couldn't believe my eyes when looking ahead toward the coast, I was able to make out a harbor full of Japanese ships, none of which had been there the day before. As we were letting down towards Wewak I also noticed on the grass runway that had been absolutely empty the day before, there were 27 Zero fighters. I had made something like 19 missions prior to this time and had never seen more than two or three fighters on this strip. Yesterday there was nothing on the field and nothing in the harbor. Yesterday's bombing mission had really been a milk run. The only enemy engagement had been that same old gunner with his three inch anti-aircraft gun sitting on top of a hill adjacent to a building that was designated as a hospital by a red cross marking on the roof. This emplacement had never been much of a problem, and I had never considered it seriously on previous raids. Today looked like an entirely different story, however, and what a target of opportunity! One lone lumbering B-24 also presented a great opportunity for the fighters on the strip and the anti-aircraft batteries on the ships in the harbor. We knew we were headed for a hot time.

We were alone and 600 miles from home base at Port Moresby, and looking down on all those goddam Japanese while supposedly flying a routine reconnaissance mission. The weather was absolutely gorgeous, sad to say for us, because we needed some cloud cover in which to hide. Tom Doyle, my bombardier, was terribly excited like everyone else, and said, through the intercom, "Mac, let's get rid of these damn bombs and get the hell out of here."

At an altitude of about 14,000 feet and about ten miles from Wewak, I turned the plane up on its side and Tom hit the salvo switch, and threw the bombs in the direction of the enemy runway. One B-24 just isn't any kind of match for 27 fighters, and a harbor full of warships. Far out at sea, there appeared to be a little bit of bad weather and I decided that it would be our salvation. I don't mind admitting that the bombs did no damage to the runway, but that didn't make any difference to us; our prime concern was getting the hell out of there. The ships in the harbor consisted of four or five transports, several destroyers and various support ships. They immediately began throwing up flak like you wouldn't believe. At the same time they were preparing to leave the harbor and had apparently unloaded their troops. Getting through all that flak wasn't my greatest concern. I was more concerned about those Zeros now zipping off the runway as fast as they could. We were at about 16,000 feet at that point. A Zero can get up to that height in about four minutes. By the time I cleared the harbor and headed out to sea for the supposedly bad weather that I hoped to hide in, I had taken a hit from flak in my No. 3 engine and the Zeroes were already attacking us. After 19 missions we had become fairly accustomed to calling out fighter approaches, but today there were so many of them that it seemed to me everyone was trying to talk over the intercom at the same time. Wynne, in the tail, was calling out three approaching Zeroes from that direction at the same time Burnett was warning me about three more attacking from above. I decided the best thing to do was to forget all their directions and make my chief concern those few blacks clouds that seemed to be about 15 or 20 miles ahead of us. They were coming at us now from above, below, from head on, from the rear and from port and starboard. We were getting the worst of it pretty fast, and in spite of any evasive action I could take, we were getting shot up badly. For the first time in my experience, I looked overhead through the plexiglass and saw a zero three or four thousand feet above me and flying my same course. I noticed he had aerial bombs under his wings, and was dropping them on me. I avoided several of his droppings, and because he didn't seem to think he was making much progress, he called his buddy up to the same altitude and they bracketed us from above. If I took evasive action to the left, the guy above me on the left would drop, and if I took evasive action to the right, his buddy would drop. These bombs had to be timed perfectly to explode on my level, which fortunately, none of them did. Most of them exploded below me. In spite of our acute anxiety, I still held hope, in the back of my mind, of getting safely into the cloud cover, and possibly from there I could duck in and out and shadow the convoy. This would certainly make me a hero if I could pull it off. By the time we reached the so-called weather, I realized how pitifully small the clouds were. I would pull into a cloud for 15 or 20 seconds and pull back out again into the clear, and the Japs must have been laughing at this pitiful maneuver. Patsy Grandolpho, my waist gunner on the left claimed our first victory of the day when he shouted through his mike that he had gotten a Zero, although I didn't see it. That was a poor swap off because now my No. 3 engine was smoking badly and I had to feather it, placing me on only 75 percent power and considerably less speed and maneuverability. Head on passes for me were the most frightening because I could see all of the action. Of course the other guys faced the same situation from their positions. The Japs would fly directly at you, firing from a thousand yards out before they rolled over and split S'ed out, barely clearing my bomb bay. Tom Doyle claimed the next one from up in the nose. It was hard for me to confirm these two kills because I was so damn busy. My co-pilot, Bob Martindale, under normal conditions was supposed to direct our firing. But being attacked by 27 enemy planes there was bedlam everywhere. Bob was doing his best to help me fly on three engines. After a few more passes, I realized how much damage had been done to my control surfaces. The ailerons and the elevators were reacting more and more slowly and the ship was getting harder to fly. Next came another group of fighters that I hadn't seen before, looking like they could hardly wait to finish me off. We think we got one more of them before my ship was flying on two engines, with all controls almost gone. We were losing altitude pretty fast and it looked as though we were going to hit the drink sooner or late, so we started preparing for it. I told the guys to get out the life jackets and for Burnett, up on the flight deck, to be ready to eject the life rafts. The plane was full of smoke and the smell of cordite was stifling. The flight deck was covered with empty 50 caliber shells. As busy as we were, there was little time to consider the hazards of a water landing. After another ten minutes of this, we were a dead duck and our time had come. Adding to our misery was a large, gaping hole in the nose from a 37 millimeter shell that had really put Tom Doyle out of commission. The explosion tore open his shoulder and left a large flap of fleshing hanging off of him, and he looked pretty damn bad to me when he came up on the flight deck. No one else had been hit as far as I knew.

We had lost most of our altitude and were now down to about

800 feet. The fighters that were still attacking, all came from above now, and if they missed us, their bullets would make rows of splashes in the water just below us. Our speed was down to around 130 mph. She stalls at 120 mph. Tracer bullets flashed past us like shooting stars. We were a fat target for these veteran pilots, most of whom had combat experience for a couple of years in China. They were the elite, as our Marine pilots were finding out down in Guadalcanal. I didn't know what the Zero's range was but some of the attackers had now gone back to Wewak, either on account of gas, or because they considered us finished. The running fight had gone on for quite a while with most of it at high speed.

As far as I knew, no one had ever ditched a B-24 in the water, as we were the first bomb group of 24's to get into combat out there. It was a high wing plane unlike a B-17 which we were told would float a little while if put down in a decent attitude.

I let the nose down a little just before we hit the water in order to build speed, then quickly raised it and gave full power so as to make as soft a flop into the water as possible. Everyone was fully aware that we were ditching. Walter Erskine, down in the nose, refused to come up onto the flight deck as Doyle and Fred Sugden, the navigator, had done. Sugden said Erskine was frozen to his 50 caliber and wouldn't leave it. Patsy Grandolpho, back in the bomb bay put on a lot of heavy flying clothes to cushion the shock of landing, I suppose.

Because of the structural design and the fat, under hanging belly, the ship broke in half on contact with the water. The guys on the flight deck, because of the heavy engines, took a nose dive straight for the bottom of the ocean. The rear section of the plane apparently floated for a couple of minutes because when I crawled out of the window, from 30 or 40 feet underwater and finally surfaced, I saw a small portion of the vertical stabilizers still above water but going down fast. The front half of the plane was near the bottom by this time, I'm sure. Burnett, the engineer, had done his job of releasing the life rafts at the moment of the crash but I quickly saw that only one raft had ejected, and it, unfortunately, was still moored to the plane by rope and was standing upright on its nose and about to be pulled under. Fred Engel, the radio

operator had also surfaced and realizing what was about to happen
to the raft, swam to it. Taking hold of the rope and reaching for
his jungle knife simultaneously he was horrified to find that he had
no knife. Screaming across the waves to Tom Doyle, 20 feet away,
Engel frantically asked Tom for his knife. Tom had also lost his
getting out of the plane. At that crucial moment Tom remembered
that he had a key chain in his pocket that also held a tiny pen knife.
His left shoulder was badly damaged but with great effort he threw
the tiny pen knife twenty feet across the water and Engel managed
to catch it and cut the rope. The raft settled back down to its
normal position and earned its appropriate name LIFE RAFT.

Months later the mental vision of a bad throw from Doyle to
Engel and the little pen knife innocently sinking hundred of feet
to the bottom of the Pacific, haunted me terribly.

Heads started popping up all around. Eight of us had escaped
the plane, but two were trapped, Grandolpho and Erskine. The
surviving raft was designed for four men, and there were eight of
us. The water was warm and the sea was calm. The quiet surface
of the ocean was such a contrast to the noise of the struggling
engines and the deafening machine gun fire we had just experienced. Swimming to the raft was effortless, considering the
alternative. Most everyone had suffered injuries from the crash,
and some of a serious nature. Before I reached the raft I realized
I still had my 45 automatic strapped to my side so I held it above
my head and out of the water to prevent rust. There were three
Jap fighters passing over and taking a last look about that time.
Doyle told me later that he thought I was firing at the Zeros. My
real intentions was to use it on each other if worse came to worse.

**B-24 Liberator – Outbound Mission**

# Chapter 4

Looking over everyone's condition, we decided which four of the crew deserved to be placed in the raft. Everyone had cuts and bruises with a considerable amount of bleeding but some were worse than others. Doyle, in addition to his wounded shoulder, had ripped the back of his right leg and a large flap of flesh about an inch thick and half the size of this page was hanging off his thigh. One of my fingers was split open and I could see the bone but others had more problems than I, so the worst four got into the raft and I and three others hung on to a rope that was tied around the edge of the raft and stayed in the water. Blood was a serious consideration as we were in the most shark infested water in the world. Everyone was in some state of shock but we did our best to get organized.

The last three Zeros were circling over head and began a power dive directly at us. This really is it, we thought, but as they zoomed fifty feet over our heads they failed to fire and simply wagged their wings and headed back toward Wewak. Later in the war, I heard that an awful lot of strafing occurred on both sides to men in the water as well as to men descending in parachutes. Thank God those pilots considered us a goner in any event.

What a lonesome feeling that was--four guys in a raft and four hanging onto it, six hundred miles from base and out of sight of land. Nevertheless, we had a pretty good rubber raft and our Mae West life preserves. We were all about 25 years old and as the saying goes, hope springs eternally, but the outlook was pretty grim; and, if you can believe, it, along about sundown, it began to look worse. The waves began building up and the fact that there was no moon didn't help our morale. The exposure to the sun earlier, our shock and our wounds had made us terribly thirsty. You would think that the raft would have been equipped with water, but it wasn't. It did have some first aid packs containing penicillin powder, and we sprinkled it over our wounds; but the water and the spray pretty much ruined that activity.

We got through the night somehow, and the sun the next morning never looked better. The surface was not too turbulent.

From time to time we would rotate getting in and out of the raft. Taking a turn in the water was done with much reluctance when on occasion we would see large fins of fish cutting across the water. They could have been sharks or porpoise or whatever, but it was not fun dangling there from the side expecting the worst. We were never attacked but were also never without great anxiety over the possible encounter with sharks. Someone up there was certainly looking out for us with at least one eye.

The second day was spent very much like the first, but we kept hoping that a B-24 reconnaissance plane might spot us since Fred Engel, our radio operator had tried mightily to contact Port Moresby and give them our position as we were being attacked by the Jap fighter planes. Unfortunately, radio reception was very poor in that area and at that distance. We saw no friendly planes and disgustedly cursed our friends for their negligence.

During the afternoon a blessed rain shower blew up and we were able not only to catch a little water to drink but got some relief from the blazing equatorial sun. Our shoes were gone and our uniforms were in tatters. The sun was murderous and our thirst was ravishing. The cool shower was most welcome until it grew into a full blown tropical storm with high winds and thunderous lightning. Gigantic waves poured over us and we bailed the water out of the raft with our hands. Those on the outside found it tough to hang onto the sides. None of us knew much about sailing, but I remembered Martindale telling us to try to head the raft into the waves to prevent capsizing. This sounded ridiculous to me, but it worked and what a roller coaster ride we had as we mounted the incoming crest and fell into the following through! I suppose there is something good in everything and the storm was no exception. It had blown us around for miles and when it abated we marveled the next morning at the sight of two small islands on the horizon. There they were; the first real hope we had had for some time. Now, if we could just get this raft going in the right direction.

The smaller island, which seemed closest to us, lay fairly low in the water and I'd guess about 15 miles away. The larger island on our right was rather hilly and loomed up out of the water maybe four or five hundred feet.

The rest of the afternoon was spent tugging and swimming and pushing and pulling and paddling with bare hands in the direction of the smaller island. The ocean currents didn't cooperate. We could make no headway. We could judge our progress or rather the lack of it by our relation to the island on the right. Someone finally suggested that if we took a 45 degree tack between the two islands we might get the benefit of a favorably current and do a land fall on the big island. It was getting dark, but we were elated to find that our guess was correct and that we were making progress on the big island. Even in the dark we could still see the silhouette of the island and the favorable current caused it to grow larger and larger, thank heaven. By midnight we believed we were going to make it. Several hours later there was no question about it. The real question was how we were going to get through the booming surf that we could see spewing up a hundred feet in the air above the rocks and coral reefs that made up the shore. What an enigma this was--land in sight, but unapproachable! Realistically, however, the terror of the surf was nothing to compare with sitting out there with no land in sight and inevitable death at sea.

There was enough light for us to be able to maneuver the raft just outside the surf, avoiding the breakers, and inspecting the shoreline. The storm was taking its toll on the island much to our regret. We've got to make that dry land no matter what the cost! So, skirting around for an hour or so we found a cove that, far from being quiet, none the less appeared to be penetrable. We said with guts and determination, let's get on with it and hit the surf. The first wave was enough to capsize the raft and send us sprawling ass over tea kettle, scattered and being raked over the jagged rocks and coral, but with luck onto dry land. It was land, but it was jungle and impenetrable; and as we individually shook off the salt water and stood erect on terrafirma, we silently breathed a prayer of thanksgiving for a measure of success and deliverance from the Pacific Ocean.

It was too much to comprehend, and in shock Martindale began wading back into the surf and later admitting that he had seen clean hospital beds and attending services out there in the water. I think it was Frank Wynne who eventually restrained him as we all collapsed into sleep just beyond the water's edge.

The booming surf and coral had taken its toll. The raft was ripped to shreds as was its crew. No one reached the shore unscratched from the vicious razor-like coral formations, most of which were just under water and impossible to see and avoid. Bare feet and knees took a beating. Some were thrown unmercifully against giant boulders and pounded again and again by the incessant waves. One by one we clawed our way to the safety of dry land, immediately collapsing into a bleeding but satisfied hulk wanting nothing more than sweet sleep. And sleep we did, from just after day break, until Farnell and I awoke sometime in the early afternoon. Without arousing anyone else the two of us decided to look around a bit and cautiously attacked the jungle barrier around us. It was so impenetrable that we only wandered 50 or 60 yards from our landing site before we gave up the effort. We saw bountiful coconut trees but didn't have the strength or ability to climb them and reach the fruit. We did find a rotten nut on the ground but were afraid to drink its milk. We could attack this problem later, but for now we were too weak. The real booster was the discovery of one lone human footprint etched in a soft mud bank. The island was at least inhabited by someone. Confident that we now had a fighting change of surviving, Farnell and I made our way back to where the others were still sleeping off the exhaustion.

In nothing flat, we, too, were out of it all and snoozing like babies until hours later when Doyle warned us in no uncertain terms, that we were surrounded by the most god awful looking Melanesian natives you ever saw. Rings in their noses, furry head bands, tattooed bodies and over all smeared with yellow powder that we recognized as our own sea marker which they had apparently recovered from our shredded raft. They approached us cautiously, spear in hand, curious as to who we were, where we had come from and what we wanted. We interpreted this strictly from signs and gestures and nothing else since they spoke only in their own language. An occasional recognizable word of Pidgin English helped us communicate that we were desperate and needed their help. Reluctantly, they approached us and condescended their assistance. Bamboo poles appeared from nowhere and when our collective Mae West preservers were fastened between parallel poles, a first class stretcher was created. One at a time the natives hauled us away from the site and into a thatched hut a mile away whose owner had moved out generously allowing the eight of us to move in, and stretch out on the bamboo slatted floor under a palm frond roof. We soon became a non-threatening curiosity and crowds of natives appeared to gape at us, some with gifts of ripe papaya and green coconut milk to drink.

Their native dialect was occasionally immersed with a word or two of Pidgin English that caught everyone's attention and was repeated over and over for clarification and with much gesturing. We succeeded in making them understand that we were not sailors but airmen whose plane had fallen in the water. We agreed on a word that sounded like "baloose" as meaning aeroplane and the verb "poundown" as meaning fall down and the word for ocean as "sali-wata." These three words made them understand; "balus poundown long sali-wata." We were helpless and at their mercy. No longer a threat to them but something of a prize possession, they promptly spread the word over the island to the several other villages along the coast, that eight strangers had miraculously appeared from the sky and were peacefully on exhibit in their village. Thirty or forty spectators passed judgement on us during the afternoon. Relaxed and fairly comfortable with far less anxiety, we slept the sleep of the innocent from sundown to sun up reveling in the comfort of a land creature in his natural habitat after an ordeal with the sea.

The first sign of opulence the next morning took the surprising form of a half a pound of vine-wrapped and thoroughly smoked pork. One of the natives presented us with this morsel as proudly as though he were offering us "Beef Wellington" and we accepted it in the same manner.

Communication was improving and we learned that there were perhaps a dozen pigs on the island and that once a year they slaughtered one and only one, smoked it and preserved it for special occasions until the next year. This was an auspicious occasion and deserved this spectacular recognition. Smoked pork, perhaps nine months old and wrapped in vines, under the circumstances was without a doubt the equal of Beef Wellington most anywhere else in the world. Gifts of papayas continued to appear for several days along with coconuts and something they called cow-cow resembling a degenerated sweet potato, not in great abundance but satisfying none the less.  As reality began to awaken in us, an assessment of our situation became necessary, and we realized that we still had a Very Pistol that could trigger our rescue from this primitive existence.  Perhaps someone back at Port Moresby would come reconnoitering the area and discover us.  Luckily it happened on the fourth day.  A lone B-24 at an altitude of about 10,000 feet skirted the island and we thought for a moment it might pass directly over us but it veered off an angle lessening the possibility of seeing us.  Throwing caution to the winds I couldn't resist the urge to fire the Very Pistol, shooting its red flare 500 feet into the air and hoping it would be seen by someone in the reconnaissance plane.  No such luck, as a matter of fact, bad luck, because the plane didn't see us and the parachute flare frightened the natives so that they deserted us for the rest of the day and we were afraid they might be disillusioned with us and withdraw their much needed support.  Adding to this letdown was the remorse I had over probably firing the one last flare prematurely.  Maybe I should have waited for a better opportunity.

On several occasions during our stay here we had noticed a somehow different looking native walking past our area. He would pass us full of sounds and gestures but refusing to look directly at us.  Instinctively, he was a desirable curiosity and we wondered what he represented.  One day as he passed by somewhat ceremoniously, one of us shouted at him in a loud voice, commanding his attention.  Facing us directly, his spell seemed to be broken and he reluctantly approached us and squatting on the ground, told us his predicament.  He was of a higher caste than our present hosts and because of his ability to do more for us he could avoid the obligation so long as he didn't look directly at us.  Now that he had seen us eyeball to eyeball, the spell was broken and he must customarily offer his superior hospitality and support.  Out of earshot of the local villagers he warned us that we were in a "place nogut" and that we should join him as guests at the village of Dop.  His name was Mot.

Mot had an official title.  He was the island Tul-Tul, which meant that he was the number two man ranked only by his chief whose name was Maligum and who was referred to as the Lulawai. His plan for the eight of us was to allow four to stay at his grass shack and the other four would stay with Maligum who lived in an adjacent village named Jop. Since he had come on foot, he decided to walk back to Dop, clear things with Lulawai and return the next day.

His departure left us with much speculation. Could Mot be trusted? Were there Japanese on the island to whom he may now be reporting our presence? If he was telling us the truth, how much of an improvement would the new villages be and especially how much more kai-kai (food) would be available to us? There was certainly no surplus kai-kai where we were although we were extremely grateful for whatever was offered.

The next day he returned in a small canoe with an outrigger and suggested that two of us go back to Dop with him and convince ourselves of the sincerity of his offer. Farnell and I volunteered to go and after a twenty minute paddle around the rocky coves and booming surf, we arrived at a landing practically in Mot's back yard. His home was very much like the one we had just left although larger and cleaner. The grass roof was supported by poles coming up from logs on which bamboo slats served as flooring. The sides were made of dried and woven palm fronds. Extending from the side of the one enclosed room was a latticed platform which was covered by the roof but had no sides. This was to be the sleeping quarters for four of us.

A shy Melanesian woman named Yap Yap and a small dark little boy of about ten years were introduced to us as Mot's wife and son Lamouche. By sign and gesture from these two who spoke no Pidgin English, Farnell and I were made to feel welcome particularly so when Yap Yap gave Mot several broad leaves of tobacco and instructions to roll us a cigar. He accommodated us promptly like a dutiful husband and presented us with a most respectable cigar. He in turn issued instructions in their native tongue for Yap Yap to bring out some food.

There always seemed to be an open fire burning around these village houses, the smell of which was rather fragrant and in addition to this now the pleasant aroma of boiling cow cow, a type of small sweet potato, got our full attention. Mot had a small cast iron pot, thoroughly blackened from years of service and perhaps dating back several generations. He tried to explain how he had come by it but the language barrier was too much for us and we could never get the story straight. Its age and design tempted us to believe it could have been a relic from Captain Cook who first sailed in these waters.

. When the cow cow had boiled in ocean water for about ten minutes, Mot added shredded coconut which Yap Yap had prepared by grating it over the serrated edge of a small sea shell. When he considered the coconut flavored cow cow sufficiently cooked, Yap Yap served them to us on a clean broad banana leaf along with a half of a giant papaya. Heaven knows where it came from because we saw no chickens, but Mot next produced a boiled hen's egg which Farnell and I eagerly divided and devoured. Another fine cigar topped off the meal and pure contentment took over for the next few hours as we happily tried to communicate with this warm primitive family. Lamouche kept a bright fire going into a starry tropical night casting flickering lights on the dark faces of our new found friends. In the background of the village street, curious but unobtrusive natives quietly observed and assessed our group. We felt secure and wanted here in Dop and gave little thought at the moment to the other six crew members on the other side of the island, which we learned was named Wageo, until peaceful sleep took its course on Mot's veranda.

The next morning after a pot of boiled taro, an adulterated Irish potato, some sac sac and ground palm heart, Mot left us and paddled off in a larger canoe to pick up the rest of our crew.

He returned with the six of them about mid morning and Farnell and I began immediately to tell them how we had spent the previous evening over a cooked meal followed by a custom made cigar.

Dop village consisted of a fairly straight row of grass huts lining each side of an open, rocky street. Both sides contained perhaps six or seven grass huts with an average occupancy of three natives. At each end of the street but set back farther into the woods were another two or three huts. The total population of the village was perhaps thirty-five men, women and children. The village of Jop where Maligum lived was not more than a half mile away with a fairly well beaten path connecting the two. Jop was almost a replica of Dop in size and construction. There was a small cemetery in each village which was set back into the surrounding greenery of palms, banana trees, and a few tropical wild flowers with bright red blossoms called ju ju by the natives. This area was well kept but seldom visited by anyone other than the person whose duty it was to keep it manicured. A few nondescript rocks without identification served as head stones.

All the huts faced the village street; an open area about a hundred feet wide. Just behind the houses however, the shrubs and trees provided pleasant shade from the equatorial sun and cool breezes rustling the leaves kept these huts comfortably air conditioned. The stately coconut trees all around the village kept the area shaded somewhat except at high noon. The ocean was no more than fifty yards from the back of Mot's house and the constant but soft sound of the surf was delightful although not quite what one normally fantasizes about south sea islands. The readily apparent poverty dispelled any preconceived fantasy of an idyllic existence of languid days and romantic nights in a wondrous land of plenty.

It was decided that Burnett, Doyle, Engel and I would accept Mot's hospitality and Martindale, Wynne, Sugden, and Farnell would move in with Maligum and his wife Wei Wei a half mile away. Maligum's son-in-law, Dal arrived about this time to welcome the entire crew and to escort the chosen four who were to be the guests of Maligum down the path to Jop and their new home.

Checking in took no time at all since the only possessions we had were the tattered clothes on our backs. There were only two pairs of shoes among the eight of us. Robinson Caruso never had it so good.

As the two groups began to get comfortably situated in their respective villages, we realized that the time had come for the next appraisal of our situation. Things now looked considerably better. We were recovered from the shock of the crash and exposure to the sun. Although we had no water, there was plenty of coconut milk to drink and we were learning to love it. We had gained the confidence of the natives and had learned to respect and trust them. We were six or seven hundred miles from our base and had no means of communication with it but were on dry land, had food to eat and were sheltered by friends.

Our first objective then was to heal our wounds and gather our strength for whatever was to come. There were no broken bones among us. Everyone had superficial cuts and bruises however, that time, if nothing else, would heal. All but Tom Doyle; his shoulder was in bad shape from the 37 m.m. shell that had exploded in the nose of the ship and to make matters worse he had ripped the back of his right thigh during the crash. He was our most serious casualty and he wasn't getting any better. We tried unsuccessfully to bandage his wounds with strips torn from our underwear. No other means of assistance was available until we made a profound discovery. Mot told us that in addition to his title of Tul-Tul he also carried the title of Doctor Boy.

We learned that this title stemmed from the fact that long ago he had sailed to Wewak and had gotten some rudimentary instructions in first aid from a Catholic nun. As time went on he obviously embellished the results of this training by assuming the title of Doctor Boy. Possessing no authentic medicine or equipment he had taken it upon himself to provide his own cures by administering whatever was available to him, consisting largely of roots and herbs immersed with a large portion of voo doo. Watching Tom suffer and our futile attempts to relieve him, Mot took the matter in his own hands and having nothing better to offer, we agreed to let him take over the case.

He gathered a conglomeration of roots and foliage, mud, dried sticks and proceeded to build up a roaring fire. He ceremoniously blessed the fire with selected sticks and much incantation. He boiled the proper leaves in his iron pot and in a most professional manner, folded the pots contents into some mud, producing a sticky consistency. The balance of the pot's contents was used to bathe Tom's wounds. Next, he administered the sticky mud pack over the wounds and covered it with clean strips of banana leaves and bound them with cord-like vines to secure the pack. After a few whistling sounds and approbation, he invited us to inspect his ministrations. We had to admit that his work looked professional and held some hope of it being efficacious. Wonder of wonders-- several days later Mot untied the vines, removed the strips of leaves and exposed a dry mud pack that was beginning to flake off the now healing wound. In another week a natural scabbing process replaced the angry flesh as it began to knit itself together along the entire gash. Mot had proved himself unquestionably to be Wageo's number one Doctor Boy and Tom Doyle's friend indeed.

It didn't seem altogether bad that the native women did most of the work. Although we never saw it, there was a small garden somewhere on top of the mountain. The women spent most of the day up there while the men mostly sat around the village amusing themselves telling stories while chewing their betel nut or simply "wokin n'about" as they put it, meaning walking around the island visiting the other villages. It was very amusing to watch these people when they encountered someone on the footpath or even in the village. They would immediately squat down on their heels at the moment of encounter, thump the gourd hanging over one shoulder and offer each other betel nut from a flat woven straw bag hanging from the other shoulder. The hollow gourd was filled with a ground white powder made from coral which has been burned in fire for many days. There was a small opening at the top of the gourd through which a long thin bone resembling a knitting needle was passed and having first been moistened in their mouth, some of the powder stuck to the needle. The combination of the betel nut and the powder in their mouth produced a red foamy saliva that the natives considered delicious. It also produced a mild intoxication. Its constant use however stained the teeth red and there were very few natives who didn't give you a broad smile exposing a full set of bright red teeth. Another physical oddity was the absence of so many big toes from their feet. How this came to be I have no idea but conservatively speaking, at least a third of all the men were missing at least one of their two big toes.

In spite of this handicap they were masters at climbing trees, particularly coconut trees. The average native man could climb to the very top of a ninety foot coconut tree in a minute flat. They accomplished this by encircling their ankles with a loop of a strong vine and clasping the trunk of the tree with both hands. Then they would bring both feet up a short distance and by exerting downward pressure, would wedge their feet to the trunk of the tree. Next they would extend their bodies upward and clutch a position several feet higher. Repeating this process they quickly reached the top where they picked the highly versatile nut and slid to the ground in a matter of seconds. The outside husk of a coconut was torn off by means of a sharp stake that had been driven into the ground. The husk produced volumes of smoke when set afire and was used to drive off mosquitoes. The milk from a green nut was slightly effervescent and delicious, and its meat was soft and sweet. The meat from a ripe nut was hard and chewy and also delicious. When dried, in the sun, oil could easily be pressed from the meat. The hard inner shell provided an excellent cup or bowl. It also was highly flammable and served as kindling as its oily fiber produced an intense heat.

In each village there was usually one native craftsman who built canoes. The quality of the finished product depended to some extent upon the careful selection of the basic log that was to be meticulously hewn over a long period of time. A canoe capable of carrying a dozen people could occupy the craftsman a year or more to complete. A simple two man canoe could be completed in a month. Much time and effort went into lashing together the long poles that served as outriggers and masts. There were no formal tools to work with but a random piece of iron had been salvaged from somewhere and fashioned into a crude axe. More primitive tools were made of pieces of sharp stone or sea shells. One of the ship builders was so adept that he carved small object of arts with these crude implements. Sails were largely made by women who wove dried strips of palm fronds into a sheet bound by pliable vines. All together the ship building rate was adequate within its rather limited requirements. Inter-island traffic was small and fishing was almost nonexistent. There was one fish hook on the island and it was Mot's treasured possession. He also had a very old fishing line that appeared rotten with age. On one occasion Mot and I paddled out into a quiet ocean cove, baited this hook with cow-cow and eventually attracted the appetite of a small fish which promptly broke the hand held line. Over the side Mot went, deftly swimming under water in pursuit of the hook and line more than for the fish. The water was clear but from above I lost sight of Mot when he was at least ten or fifteen feet below the surface. After what seemed to me to be at least five minutes, Mot triumphantly broke the surface with hook, line and fish in tow. Wrapped in wet salty leaves and baked in the coals of an open fire, this two pound fish was a gourmet's delight and the topic of conversation for several days.

One clear day when several of us were rambling around the island at its higher elevation we could see the tip of another island on the distant western horizon. We had seen two small islands to the S.E. of us, but this one was only visible on a clear day from the higher levels of Wageo. Asked what it was, Mot surprised us by giving its name as Kariru and adding that there was a missionary on it whose name we concluded was something like Fodda Manun, a Catolik. A catholic missionary named Father Manion! What luck! We descended on Mot like bees with all sorts of questions, very little of which was understood or answered. It made no difference to us, we had reason to rejoice.

For the next few days we though of nothing but Father Manion probably sitting over there with a short wave radio or perhaps a schooner of some sort. Magnanimous as he was, Mot eventually acceded to our constant entreaty and agreed to select three crewmen and sail to Kariru.

From the Wageo shore line, Kariru could not be seen. It was quite a distance away and the voyage was not to be taken lightly but Mot found his crewmen in a few days and lots of excited islanders pitched in to help Captain Mot with his preparations. A fresh new sail was woven, new paddles were hewn and the lashings on the chosen outrigger were renewed. Friends brought select green coconut and fresh taro for the voyage. Gifts of tobacco and betel nut were generously provided and as the boisterous excitement reached a pitch, the four black Melanesians shoved off.

Their departure had been delayed somewhat by their innate ability to predict the weather. They would not attempt the long voyage until the wind was right. The right wind they waited for was called Telleo. Telleo would eliminate paddling. Their return trip would require a Rye wind to be successful.

Just prior to leaving I gave Mot a small capsule made from a joint of bamboo into which I had placed a note to the mythical Father Manion. Someone had salvaged a pencil and the note was scribbled on a pliable piece of fiber that was quite legible. Now we had done all we could do and the rest was up to our great benefactor, the Tul-Tul of Wageo.

Anticipation mounted daily as we awaited Mot's return with the good news and quick deliverance. Each day seemed an eternity in his absence. A week went by, then two weeks. Rain and foul weather dampened our spirits.

Lamouche and I vainly tried to communicate each morning before he disappeared to God knows where with the other children. One fine morning as we babbled incoherently at each other gesturing wildly over some mutual discovery, we were interrupted rudely by the sounds of several blasts on a conch shell. Its intensity increased and all movement in the village street came to a halt. Several more blasts on the conch signaled a message that turned the quiet village street into frenzied turmoil.

Everyone in sight left what they were doing and began running down a path that led to the ocean. It was about nine o'clock in the morning and never had I seen so much action. I interrupted an acquaintance and holding him by the arm asked what was going on--"Whanin sumting long conch?" "Mot i cum bak" was the answer. I joined the running crowd and arrived at the rocky beach to gaze out on an empty ocean. Nothing in sight--I questioned the gathering crowd again and again, "Sali-wata i gut nating, whanim sumting?" There's nothing out there, why are you excited? "Mot i cumbak" was the stock reply. My crew and I in hopeful disbelief retired after an hour or so, to a shady spot overlooking the ocean and gradually convinced ourselves that these primitive people were out of their minds. Mot was no where to be seen out on that ocean.

The afternoon drug on and still no sign of a canoe. The natives however were adamant and stuck to the shore line. Night fell slowly over the western horizon. Engel gave a half hearted, self-consoling shout, "There he is just to the left of the setting sun!" Rubbish. Just your imagination. The equatorial stars came out ever so brilliantly. None of the natives left the beach except to quickly find a bread fruit somewhere and return to take up his observation post overlooking the sea.

New Guinea native enjoying betel nut.

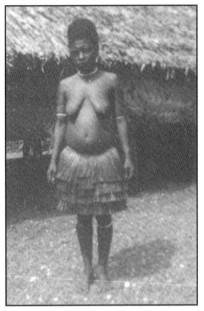

Our Hostess, Yap Yap

Sepic River native smoking
bamboo pipe.

Citizens of Jop

# Chapter 5

A weary but enthusiastic welcoming party bolted upright when the unquestionable silhouette of a large canoe became visible on the star-lit-water sometime after midnight. When it reached a point no more than a couple of hundred yards from shore we nervously realized that this was not the canoe that had left Wageo but was much larger and instead of a crew of four there were 15 or 20 people aboard. As it drew even nearer, I was very pleased to make out the beautiful form of a thoroughbred Irish Setter. Without a doubt that meant that Father Manion was aboard. No native ever owned such a creature, but it wasn't until the canoe landed that sadly I realized there was no white man amongst the passengers. This was something of a let down, but we hadn't talked to Mot yet because of all the back-slapping, embracing and renewing of old acquaintances among the natives. The additional passengers turned out to be former citizens of Wageo returning home after being away several years.

Mot in his usual diplomatic fashion greeted us warmly showing no sign of the news he bore. He insisted that everyone go home and get a good night's sleep and gather at his house for a meeting the next morning.

Mot convened the meeting with words I'll never forget. A sympathetic smile betrayed the words I knew he was going to utter "Sore long yu fella, Masta Jamis." He went on to tell the crestfallen group that Kariru was completely occupied by Japanese soldiers. They were everywhere and some of them even slept on the ground, "olosem pig." We learned that there was a Catholic mission station on Kariru with a rather large contingent of priests, brothers, sisters, nuns and even a Bishop. The missionaries were being treated dreadfully by the soldiers. Several had been killed and the Bishop himself had been bayoneted, although not fatally. They had been herded into a compound, Father Manion among them, and communication with them was very guarded. The missionaries were allowed very little contact with the natives, most of whom were forced into labor gangs.

Incredulously, Mot had been able to slip up to the compound

and toss my capsule over the wire to Father Manion in the middle of the night. This was a dangerous thing for Mot to do and equally dangerous for Manion to be caught collaborating with Mot. Manion's immediate reaction, knowing the conditions under which we were living on Wageo, was for Mot to advise us to come to Kariru or nearby Wewak and give ourselves up to the Japanese. He concluded that there was no escape possible for us since the Japs controlled the entire north coast of New Guinea through which we would have to pass in order to get back to Port Moresby on the south coast and over the Owen-Stanley Mountains, 600 miles away.

In addition to his contact with Father Manion he surreptitiously made our situation known to some other contingent of the Mission who was bold enough to prepare a gift of essentials composed of paper, iodine crystals, two bars of soap, a few feet of rope, a couple of butcher knives and a cooking pot. All of these gifts, Mot humbly presented to us and left the decision of our next move squarely on our laps.

To a man, our decision was unanimous, Father Manion had to be out of his mind. There were worse things then eating coconut and papaya and coexisting with stone age natives. We would sweat it out with our friends as long as they would tolerate us.

Wageo was divided. Toleration was up in the air. Some of the natives loved us, some were more practical. What would happen to them if the Nips came over and found them aiding and abetting the enemy? Debate evolved in the village street night after night. Mot, our champion, was eloquent. So were the dissenters, a strong case on either side. Mot lost gracefully, with a little cooperation from the eight American airmen who began more and more to realize that we were a hot potato that should not jeopardize the safety of innocent bystanders. Our minds were made up--we would leave.

We spent the next few days preparing for a hazardous overwater trip, island hopping off shore from the second largest island in the world, New Guinea. ultimately we would have to land on the big island which was infested not only with Japanese soldiers, but with a healthy population of crocodiles, pythons, adders, malarial mosquitoes and torrential rivers. In order to trek back to Port Moresby, our only allied base, we were faced with crossing the Owen-Stanley mountain range. One of those mountains, Mt. Wilhemina at times is covered with snow at its highest elevation and its location is no more than 3 or 4 degrees south of the equator (180 miles). The interior natives on the whole were a great deal more uncivilized and hostile. We queried every native that had ever sailed to the south and east of Wageo for information. The Lulawai was more informative than any one else as he could have been 70 or 80 years old and was full of native intellect. He proposed that we be escorted by 6 Wageo natives in their finest canoe down to the island of Koil with a pit-stop in route at the small island of Wei. This could be done in one day. The Wageo natives could return and he would send word for the Koil natives to escort us to Blup Blup and from there to Katovar and from there to the mouth of the Sepic River on Big New Guinea. His authority as Lulawai allowed him to command the services of other island natives in our behalf.

The departure of good friends from the island population with all its sad "good-byes" reminded Maligum and Mot of another occasion perhaps twenty years earlier when, as they related, a Masta Hobin had visited them, charmed them and ultimately had had to bid them good-bye. I learned later that this episode related to a study that was made by an eminent Australian anthropologist named Hogbin from Sydney University. This scientist had evidently been dropped off by schooner on the island, made a study of people and their civilization and returned to the university after the completion of a research project.

As our departure time drew near, I asked Mot and Yap Yap, Maligum and Wei Wei to meet with me and my crew for a conference. I still maintained the pencil someone had salvaged from the crash, and with it I penciled our legacy to the marvelous people of the village of Dop and Jop. To the best of my memory the message said:

*"To whom it may concern: To the everlasting credit for the loyalty, friendship and generosity of the people of the village of Dop and Jop of the Island of Wageo, I, Lieut. James McMurria and*

*my aircraft crew of seven, consisting of Martindale, Doyle, Sugden,*
*Wynne, Burnett, Engel and Farnell do hereby bequeath 22 pounds,*
*Australian currency, two wrist watches, a U.S. Army 45 caliber*
*automatic pistol (rusty), four U.S. Army dog tags and two gold*
*rings. Signed......James A. McMurria 0372644 USAAF*

These amenities having been duly observed, my crew and I
proceeded to the beach where Wageo's finest crew and canoe was
assembled for the final farewells.

Maligum addressed the crowd of well wishers that had
gathered there, in his own language, being interpreted into Pidgin
by Dal, his son-in-law for our benefit. He told them about the
presents we had left and announced that it would be "Kanadia" or
something for all. He spoke kindly to us and blessed us in his own
manner and suggested that we shove off. Several women began to
cry a little and the children struck up a song. Yap Yap became
emotional and left the scene in disarray.

We hopped into the coconut laden canoe with the six Kanakas
at the paddles and proceeded for about 50 yards when a commotion
arose and we came about for the shore again. Old Maligum who
hadn't left the island for year had suddenly decided he would take
probably his last voyage and at the very last minute wanted to
accompany us down as far as Koil. A young boy was dispatched
to his house to fetch some equipment for the trip and behold, he
returned with an ancient umbrella. Several strong men waded out
*into the water in an effort to* get the blind Lulawai comfortably
seated in the forward part of the canoe. At last we were off to see
something more exciting than the Wizard of Oz.

# Chapter 6

We were sad to leave those friendly pint sized black people. We were fully aware of the ominous route that hopefully would take us back to our allies. The obstacles would be many and the success in grave doubt but now out on the open water with a fresh wind in our face and a crew of six strong men enthusiastically paddling, we took heart and joined the jubilant spirit of the crew. With the raising of the sail, a good salt spray blowing up and a swig of coconut juice right from the nut, I was suddenly Fletcher Christian, Ulysses and Noah all wrapped up in one, but secretly was also "lifting up mine eyes unto the hills, from whence cometh my help" I hoped.

It only took fifteen minutes for us to make our first mistake. We looked back at Wageo thus breaking a cardinal native rule-- never look back once under way! We were gently chastised for our breach of policy and dependant as we were on their beneficence it never happened again. Basically, the canoe itself was not more than a large 30 foot log, painstakingly hewn and carved in a design handed down from generations of semi-seafaring Melanesians. They gave little evidence of being the sailors that the Polynesians are credited with being. However, they sailed the short inter-island ocean voyages and rivers with confidence and efficiency. Like all native outriggers ours consisted of three symmetrical poles forming a "U" with the open ends being lashed to the sides of the canoe by strong vines and the closed end bearing a small section of a buoyant log off the port side. Being fairly oval in shape, the canoe would readily capsize without the leverage balance of the outrigger. Ours rode comfortably over the swells and falls of the galloping surface of the water. The lashings creaked and moaned as they rose and fell with the swells but never gave hint of insecurity. When the sail was up and full, the ocean foam flew happily past us in crazy quilt design and we marveled at the speed. Without the wind, the six crewmen paddled prodigiously unmindful of the weight of their six foot paddles or the energy expended. In a sustained calm the wind-master took charge. The designated crewman would stand erect in the canoe, position his conch shell and give forth with loud blasts designed to attract a favorable wind. Intermittently, he would lower his conch and make verbal incantations to the wind saying "Cum, cum cum big fella, big fella, big fella mo, cum big fella win." It worked marvelously and the sail would be hoisted again to everyone's delight.

Maligum was the central figure with his umbrella and was enjoying the voyage immensely. With a sly sense of humor he passed the word to me through others that he was very sorry for me in that I was going to make fine kai-kai for the interior natives on New Guinea. Kai-kai was their word for food and we had heard rumors of cannibalism of the wild Kukukus and Chimbu tribes in the mountains. Maligum admitted that he had never eaten human flesh but that his father was a devotee of it, advising that if one stood on a hill overlooking two valleys, one having a man cooking pig and the other cooking human flesh, the aroma of the latter would inevitably draw you in its direction. He would then jokingly pinch me on the thigh with, "Oh Masta Jamis, you numba wun kai-kai."

Maligum's little joke was amusing to everyone but the eight of us. "Come on now Lulawai, tell us the truth. The days of cannibalism are all gone, aren't they?"--He wasn't sure. Along the coast we should be okay but the interior was a different matter and it had been years since he had visited the big island. Judging by looks alone would lead you to believe that they were all cannibals.

The canoe cut the foaming water marvelously well and the sea spray and ocean air was exhilarating. High adventure rode with us at easily five or six knots per hour; so that by mid day we were approaching our first check point, the island of Wei. I imagined we would stretch our legs a little here and take a look at Wei, but that wasn't the game plan. Instead, three fine looking native men greeted us at the shore and promptly joined us in the canoe. It was a mystery to us that this all seemed to be prearranged. How did they know we were coming and who informed them to be ready to join us for the last leg of the trip down to Koil? It served no purpose to pry into their affairs so we let well enough alone and asked no questions. Wei didn't look too inviting in the first place, being rather rock strewn and hilly so it was no disappointment when we shoved off immediately with three additional crew men. Their added strength on the oars quickly propelled us out into a stiff breeze to the joy of these born sailors. The newcomers were jovial and chartered incessantly with their Wageo friends obviously about the eight white men aboard.

Along with the coconuts and cow cow in the floor of the canoe were many branches of palm trees under which we intended to hide in case inquisitive Jap aircraft or vessels were encountered. Fortunately this did not become necessary and we sped along under full sail most of the way down to Koil Island and the natives enjoyed the relief from paddling. Just outside the breakers on the southwest side of the island we ran out of wind and the crew began to paddle leisurely around the undulating contour of the coast. As we rounded a prominent cove, Maligum spoke rapidly in his native dialect as if he were telling a story. Although he was blind, he seemed to know exactly where he was and he began pointing toward a part of a small cliff containing a curious looking stone. Mot interpreted the story in Pidgin for us. The stone was a monument that had been crudely chiseled into a symmetrical design and was full ten feet in length, breath and depth and must have weighed tons. Maligum said that the monolith had been brought from Wageo and given to the Koil natives as a peace offering years before he was born. Two mysteries evolved. How did Maligum know its position since he was blind and how was it ever transported to Koil? Again it was not ours to doubt or question so we silently marveled at these primitive, paradoxical people.

From the outskirts, Koil was lovely. There were sandy beaches nestled in quiet coves rimmed with clear blue and aquamarine Pacific water--cool, palm shaded lagoons. A variety of colorful jungle flowers rejoiced in the pale shadows of large acacias and d'albertis. Banana trees bore fruit which was not the case on Wageo. A thoroughly inviting island on which we would have been pleased to take up a lengthy residence under other circumstances.

A hundred natives waded or swam out to greet us in the warm shallow water of a broad beach. Old acquaintances embraced from the gunnels of the canoe. Children raced on the sandy beach and elderly women waved a cheery welcome. Everyone seemed to know old Maligum but gregarious Mot was the central figure among the new arrivals while a boisterous native named Joko was preeminent among the receiving party.

A surprisingly acceptable feast of native fruit and vegetables awaited us in a neat little village just a few hundred yards inland. Hospitality was rampant although slightly overdone by some who generously transferred a wet sloppy cigarette from their own mouths forcefully into ours. Surviving this ordeal with no lethal results we, in the festive spirit of things, decided to try betel nut.

We doused our mouths with an appropriate amount of the ground coral powder, from someone's gourd, popped in a green betel nut and began to chew. Effervescent foam immediately brewed up in abundance. The acrid and bitter-sweet flavor of the concoction met mixed reactions. Sugden and Engel rather like it, but the rest of us found it mildly objectionable; all but Burnett, who retracted in horror to the great amusement of Joko and his coterie.

Our plan of escape spread quickly among the Koilites who received the news rather sadly among themselves. They didn't think we had much chance of getting back to Port Moresby by over the rugged mountains and past the Japanese guarding the coast. They had just learned from Mot of the Japanese presence and of the atrocities being committed on Kariru among the missionaries.

Joko was adamant. He would have none of it. We should stay there on Koil, enjoy the beautiful island and live a life of ease as he did. He could arrange a bride for each of us if we so desired and we could live out our days with him. The idea was appealing, all but the bride, but reality demanded that we move on with our escape plan and shoot for Blup Blup the next day.

The feast over, we prepared for bed and ensconced ourselves comfortably on a woven straw pallet resting on a bed of soft leaves.

The white hot sun rose quickly out of the eastern ocean the next morning scattering thin wisps of red and yellow stratus clouds that were the remnants of the night's huge cumulus formations. Near the equator towering clouds build up over land as the heat of the day progresses. At night the process reverses and the build up occurs over the ocean to mature at 40 and 50 thousand feet and dissipate before daybreak leaving colorful airborne ribbons to greet the morning sun.

We arose early knowing that we had a full schedule ahead of us and that today we would say good-bye to one of the greatest friends of a lifetime, Mot the Magnificent. He had saved our skins in so many ways, he had engineered our voyage thus far and was now busily instructing the new crew of Koil natives who would sail us down to Blup Blup in their canoe while he returned to Wageo.

When the new crew and the provisions were loaded and it was time to leave, Mot and I faced each other blankly. How can I express the depth of gratitude I felt for this lovable man in native patois? My soul was linked to his and he shared it. Unashamedly, we embraced for a long minute, tears welling up in our eyes. Mot capped the emotion with "we all same baby!" I released him, turned my back and waded out to the canoe, never to see him again in this world; but, at least, somehow in the next.

Our new shipmates were sympathetic enough with our case but being new found friends, to some extent were impersonal. Let's have a good adventurous sail down to Blup Blup, a day on the water, a night away from home, an acceptable cause and under the auspices of the Lulawai of Wageo. If the new crew was a bit frivolous, their seamanship didn't reflect it. This was a long voyage requiring good navigation, favorable winds, hours of rugged paddling during calms and sound judgment in after dark maneuvering through treacherous rocks and shoals bordering our objective, mountainous Blup Blup. With considerable night time haze and no moon, we whizzed through protruding coral reefs and giant boulders that were eager to capsize us and deliver us to the profusion of sharks often visible before the sun went down. At first sight, our port was incredulous, a narrow gap between two huge rocks with just enough passage for the canoe and outrigger terminating at the base of a steep cliff. There was no anchorage what-so-ever and the bow of the canoe had to be hauled up ten feet or more vertically against the cliff to secure it. No one greeted us until we had climbed 300 or 400 feet straight up and burst upon an unlit, bedraggled group of impoverished shacks and a few emaciated tenants, a sorrowful sight, completely defusing our enthusiasm over making port through treacherous waters.

Our crew conversed quietly and unenthusiastically in the dark with the small gathering of Blup Blupites. A few skimpy sweet potatoes were offered somewhat begrudgingly, and with no further accommodations forthcoming, we gloomily looked for a soft, dry spot to sleep and in no time at all there wasn't a sound to be heard other than the eerie calls of various night birds. Everyone slept nervously and was wide awake at the crack of dawn in time to see hundreds of huge flying foxes awkwardly returning across the dim water to the forest after their nocturnal feeding, God knows where. The fur of these fruit bats was highly prized by the natives, who fashioned head bands out of it, but the ungainly flapping of their black angular wings in the dim light of dawn or dusk set a rather melancholy mood for the day to come.

Without fanfare, the Koil natives returned to their canoe and left us, friendless, in an impoverished and impersonal environment. The rather dwarfed crew that was ordained to carry us to Catavar had unkempt beards and a generally disheveled appearance. Their canoe projected a similar image. This island, having no semblance of a harbor, no doubt suffered economically from a lack of native trade and accounted for its insolvency, along with the acid sterility of its soil. We climbed down the precipitous cliff over a gnarled tangle of rocks and roots to the canoe standing upright against the cliff.

The new crew was stoic; efficient but disinterested. We hardly spoke during the long hours of intermittent sailing in brisk winds and equatorial clams. With Catavar in sight on the horizon, spirits rose in anticipation of a better reception and an improved atmosphere. Even the crew seemed relieved with their objective now in sight. Approaching mountainous Catavar, in the distant haze to our right ominous New Guinea loomed faintly. We began to speculate that Catavar would be a real turning point for us. Because of its proximity to the Jap held New Guinea coast, these people surely would know the situation on the big island. Tensions were mounting.

Two old Kanakas waded out to assist the stiff, bone weary, but anxious voyagers. A cacophony of native dialect ensued. Two more old islanders appeared surreptitiously from the shadows beyond the rocky harbor. Discord was apparent but its source was a mystery to us; nevertheless, we were led hesitantly to their village and given a little taro and an abundance of unappetizing bread fruit. Their distended stomachs and tenia ridden bodies was a sorry sight. Fully half of them were suffering from great ulcerated tropical yaws around their ankles. Pitifully undernourished and naked children stared wild eyed at us. Communication was almost nil, and yet unthreatening. The Blup Blups delivered their message and were gone. A new crowd held our destiny.

Walking barefoot around the village, my waning confidence was smitten by the sight of a canvas shoe. It was unmistakenly Japanese. A pocket for the big toe was divided from the rest of the shoe like a catcher's mit. I also saw a weather worn box inscribed with Japanese characters. Both items were most likely flotsam from a sunken ship, but how could we be sure?

After a restless night on this forlorn rock, it was time to take the big step to New Guinea itself. The mild rain we encountered worked both for us and against us. Obstructions to visibility would protect our approach from prying eyes on shore, but the choppy water whipped up by the tropical rain was a threat to the dilapidated canoe whose outrigger was less than effective. Only two natives manned the boat, either because of the short distance to be traveled or by a lack of volunteers.

A choppy swell spilled over both sides of the canoe when we were about half way to shore, swamping us and practically shearing off the outrigger. We held onto the canoe, floating just under water and drifted with the current. An incoming tide saved us after several hours in the water and delivered us gingerly onto a broad sandy beach. This whole experience had not been too frightening since, from possibly five miles off shore, we found the water was rather shallow and at times we could touch bottom; the result, we gathered, of the enormous flow of silt brought down by the Sepic River drainage several miles east of where we came ashore. Maligum was right, Catavar was opposite the mouth of this giant river. Approaching the shore from several miles out, we had noticed a wisp of smoke rising from the beach just south of where we had landed. The Catavar natives assured us the smoke came from a Kanaka's fire and after landing they readily agreed to walk down the beach and investigate the source, leaving the eight of us alone on a big New Guinea beach with no further native contact.

A sketchy briefing from Maligum back on Wageo told us that close to the mouth of the Sepic we would find two villages, both under his jurisdiction, and the each would offer succor if his name was mentioned. How to find these villages was now our biggest concern. Dark was approaching. Just beyond the beach lay the vast swampland everywhere ridden with greasy dank mud, tangled mangroves and crocodile infested pools. Around the muddy pools grew slimy bushes covered with phosphorescent fungi dimly glowing with an unearthly spectral light after dark. Mosquitoes and a multitude of other insects clouded the air like smoke above the swamp.

The wet land was too hazardous to attack after dark, so we milled around on the beach hoping our crewmen would return with some information as to how to reach the nearest village. Presently we saw two natives coming up the beach; one was a crewman and the other a stranger. Instinctively I was suspicious of the stranger. He was smoking a pipe that was definitely a manufactured product and looked vaguely oriental. He told us there were no Japanese in the area, which was certainly good news, but our confidence in him was blown when Wewak was mentioned and he offered in good faith to escort us west to that enemy stronghold. Now the cat was out of the bag and our suspicions were confirmed.

We had no alternative, as the native disappeared into the night, but to remain there on the beach until daylight. Our bodies were fairly comfortable, since the breezy beach was without mosquitoes or insects, but our mind were filled with anxiety. Sugden and Engel engaged in a lot of jargon filled rhetoric typical of the professional optimism with which both were blessed. The rest of us viewed our situation with increasing alarm. We sprawled out on the beach in search of sleep that might brighten our spirits when this uneasy night was over.

Most everyone was up at least once during the night for one reason or another with nervousness being the chief cause. I found the gusty wind on the hard sand annoying so I tried stretching out on the floor of the canoe whose sides would knock the wind off me. Palm leaves in the canoe were a little bit of a cushion and I was able to sleep fairly comfortably most of the night.

Burnett aroused me sometime close to daybreak saying that he had heard suspicious noises just off the beach. I tried to assure him that if anything at all, there might be curious natives in the area looking us over. Frank Wynne reported hearing similar noises. Mustering false confidence, I told them to go back to sleep which they attempted after meandering around in the dark for a few minutes.

I heard no more from them but found I couldn't sleep either. Knowing how close we were to a major enemy installation, the alien beach adjoining that forbidding jungle was making a coward out of me. This has to be just a bad dream, I thought.

I calculated and recalculated our chance of success-winking starlight seemed to be laughing at me accentuated by wind-blown sand spraying intermittently into the canoe. I fought a negative intuition that enveloped me like a shroud. I thought of the wet canoe as a coffin soon to be attacked by droves of sand crabs and vultures completing the cycle and returning my bloated body to the sea--the unfulfilled ambitions, my sins and my obligations. The frenzy of the crash into the ocean hadn't given me time to consider these things. My whole life hadn't flashed before me as is sometimes reported in these situations. Here it was different--I had the rest of that night for reflection--exhaustion eventually over ruled pessimism and I fell asleep.

B-25 (90th Bomb Group) – Typical low level attack against Japanese war ship.

# Chapter 7

Just as the upper crescent of a fire red sun broke the seascape to the east I was awakened by ungodly, frantic screaming and much milling about.  A patrol of about twenty Japanese soldiers were bearing down on us in full stride with bayonet mounted, rifles at the thrust.  They had hidden in the thick brush just off the beach sometime during the night and had waited until daylight to mount a screaming bonsai charge completely surrounding us.  There didn't seem to be an officer among them.  A scrawny, unkempt non-com seemed to be in charge.  He repeatedly shouted orders half in Japanese and half in broken English--"If you run, I shoot kill.  No run, I shoo kill."  The rest of the patrol made threatening gestures with their bayonets at each of us.  The frenzied, almost insane activity of these dumpy little guys promoted me to calmly advise my crew to be very still and silent since the Nips were unquestionably trigger happy.

Unexplainably, a sense of calm did come over me.  Perhaps my conception of Japan as a civilized nation, certainly as contrasted with our recent stone age experience, led me to believe we were at least about to come back into the twentieth century.  I was soon to learn that the conjecture was highly debatable.

(Not withstanding) the fact that we were becoming prisoners, I was, in a way glad we would no longer be exposed to the elements, nor have to survive on coconuts and bread fruit.  Our prospects looked bad but nevertheless somewhat improved.

The soldiers continued to rush around screaming at us and at each other in complete disorder.  We were understandably docile in our bare feet, unarmed and in rags.  They were heavily armed and properly equipped for he jungle environment--soft canvas shoes, wrapped leggings, light weight ammo belts and caps with a flap extending down to the shoulders to protect against mosquitoes and the sun.  Their rifles were about three quarters the size of our M-1, befitting of their own short statue.  Their bayonets, however were extremely long in relation to the length of the rifle.

It soon became evident that these people weren't your

University types but thoroughly dedicated peons of the Emperor, thrust into a situation of responsibility beyond their narrow conception. We were posing no threat and offering no resistance, yet they appeared more frightened than we did. This was an awesome occasion for coolies not many moons out of the rice paddy. From that standpoint, things looked advantageous for the moment but soon proved otherwise. When dominating a water buffalo constitutes the limit of one's experience, it's unreasonable to expect a silk purse out of a sow's ear.

Through mime and gesture they demanded that we lie flat on the beach and submit to being tied hand and foot with fine sisal twin which restricted circulation. Next, they extended two heavy manilla ropes, one around the chest and one around the knees, through which they placed a strong bamboo pole that allowed a man at each end to carry us suspended like a dead north woods deer for several miles down the beach and into their jungle outpost. The trip took over an hour during which time they stopped twice to rest and smoke cigarettes. We enjoyed the rest more than they did as it relieved the pressure of the ropes. They seldom spoke to each other and not at all to us as they stoically padded along in their uniforms dripping with sweat.

Our personality boy Engel made several attempts at conversation which I called suspended animation, to the effect of:

"Come on you guys, let's have a little rest and a cigarette." He was rewarded with several brutal kicks and a mock bayonet thrust. Conversation ceased.

Their camp consisted of three or four crudely constructed platforms set up on logs that supported a roof that was part corrugated metal and thatch. Mosquito netting formed the four sides. There was a rock lined dugout for fires, several black iron cooking pots and an oil drum filled with fresh water--vine filled trees completely shut out the sun.

Upon arrival we were untied and allowed to stretch and massage our slightly swollen wrists and ankles, then placed on a platform with no roof or netting. Two guards stood watch constantly. There was no restriction on conversation, but they never tried to communicate with us and seldom spoke to each other. It was difficult to see clearly into their quarters due to the mosquito netting, but occasionally when someone lifted it to enter or exit we could see articles of clothing and straw mats resting on canvas sacks obviously filled with leaves or some other soft materials. Our bed was the slatted floor of the platform whose cracks made it very uncomfortable, however there was just enough room for us to stretch out.

At the end of our first miserable day as prisoners, so far without food, there was much speculation as to when and what we would be fed. A small fire and several pots were being tended by a shirtless soldier wearing a small towel as a head band to absorb his abundant perspiration. The rapid chopping noises he was making and the boiling pots triggered the Pavlovian response in spades and brightened our dull spirits. Alas, it was not for us- - we were handed a carefully measured ball of white rice, unsalted and rudely delivered after they finished their evening meal with much burping and sucking of their profusion of gold teeth.

Tom Doyle rationalized, "These people are just out-post pickets who are cut off from the main supply lines- -they don't have much food themselves. Wait til we get with the main body and we'll have regular Japanese army rations."

"Yeah, I think I'll wait," said Sugden, the venerable school teacher turned navigator. "From the looks of the guard's rifle, I deem it propitious." "You're not really hungry are you, Bob?"

Bob Martindale rolled his eyes in disgust and didn't answer.

"Well, you can roll your eyes and clam up and pout if you want to, but we wouldn't be in this mess if you hadn't voted to leave Wageo against my better judgment," taunted Engel, who had wanted to stay on with the natives. He and Farnell loved Wageo and had a particular attachment to a native couple who had a baby while we were there and named it Farnell.

Bob shrugged his shoulders and closed his eyes in utter

disregard for what he considered insubordination from an enlisted man.

Big Tom Doyle just moaned a little moan and told everybody to shut up--his shoulder and thigh wound still wasn't healed in spite of Mot's ministration and the vicious ropes on the trip down the beach and into the camp site hadn't helped his wounds very much--I was speculating our future and didn't want to get into the controversy.

A highly mosquitoey night ensued. We were used to sleeping without a pillow but sleep was almost impossible due to dejection, excessive fatigue and of course, insects. During the night the stoic guards standing at "parade rest" seemed so worn out from duty that they, from time to time, would fall asleep while standing up and barely catch themselves before they actually fell--apparently they had stayed awake all the previous night while we slept on the beach.

At daybreak two relieving guards came on duty and the commotion awakened those of us who were lucky enough to have been asleep and speculation about breakfast became our paramount concern. A repetition of last night's fiasco ensued--another rice ball grudgingly presented, followed by a heated discussion among the Japanese obviously concerning their next move.

Two soldiers meticulously dressed themselves and departed on an obviously important mission. A slightly more relaxed atmosphere among them gave us reason to believe that our captors were now very confident and proud of themselves and were as anxious to spread the news of their success as they were to get rid of a hot potato. Eight hot potatoes.

After their departure two obsequious and smiling Kanakas appeared from the bush profusely thanking the remaining Japanese for the gift of several yards of rope, their reward for our betrayal. One smoked an oriental pipe- -Judas, no doubt. A bad conscience wouldn't allow either of the natives to so much as glance in our direction.

At mid-morning the two guards returned accompanied by a

Gunso (a Japanese army sergeant), and two additional privates. The Gunso commanded great respect from the others as he went about his business of formally taking control of us and preparing to move us out to another location. We were handcuffed but not tied up and marched about two miles on a jungle trek to a small river where a 20 foot inboard motor boat was tied up. Certain insignia and a cross on its forecastle identified it as having belonged to missionaries. We moved up river for twenty minutes before entering the much larger waters of the Sepic River. Another half hour up the Sepic and we arrived at a well constructed dock that harbored two military landing barges. Approximately a hundred Japanese service people of all types crowded the dock inquisitively. Word had spread of our expected arrival. We were not derided in any way but simply starred at in stony silence. We surmised that their discipline was due to the presence of an officer who promptly took charge from the Gunso and issued orders for a ration of rice and salted pickles to be given us. The officer spoke only a little English, but introduced us to an interpreter named Watanabi.

Tom Doyle smiled and commented softly, "Now we're getting somewhere. This doesn't look so bad, does it? Let's see what Watanabi has to say."

Watanabi overhead him and promptly addressed us. "You are now in the hands of the Imperial Japanese Army. Japan is making war against the United States as part of the South East Asia Co-Prosperity Program. None of you speak Japanese so I advise you to learn the language as best you can and as fast as you can since you will be under Nippon jurisdiction for the rest of your lives."

"Humph" retorted one of us who was promptly glared at by the interpreter with an utterly sinister smile.

"You are a disgrace to your country and the fact that you are still alive is because of the noble Japanese Bushido Code, which you do not understand. It has many facets and your existence in this world will depend on your adherence to its tenets," Watanabi cautioned. "Lieutenant Asai is now your commander and he will speak to you through me as we leave this place by barge to join his Majesty's unconquerable forces at Wewak."

Lieutenant Asai looked considerably less belligerent than the dozen or so men who joined us in the landing barge. It was comforting to know he was in charge.

For several hours we made our way up various tributaries of the Sepic during which time Asai asked us many questions. He wanted to know at what altitude barges could best be seen from the air? Was their brush camouflage effective? Had we bombed many barges, etc.? Our answers invariably reflected our ignorance and innocence with an eye on the rear of the barge where food was stored.

This rather amicable parley was abruptly discontinued as night approached. The barge pulled over and stopped at the mouth of an inlet leading out into the ocean. A muffled conference took place in the rear of the barge out of earshot. Orders were given to bind us again hand and foot very tightly with something like telephone wire. They then carried us to the extreme front of the barge which portion was well above the water line and could be lowered or raised for whatever purpose was necessary. The eight of us lay prostrate squarely in the center of the collapsible section of the bow in excruciating pain from the wire binding our ankles and wrist. Any whimper or request for relief was answered with the butt of a rifle or the toe of a boot.

The barge plowed its ways several miles out into the ocean, its engine alternating from low to high pitch as the propeller regularly came out of the water and spun in free air. A high wind and cold ocean spray produced shivering spasms in our nearly naked bodies.

God fearing Leslie "Smiley" Burnett, the innocent blue eyed straight arrow from Rocky Mount, N.C., the best aircraft engineer in our 90th Bomb Group, murmured prayers for us all.

"This is it, boys, they're gonna dump us off this platform. It may as well be now as later. I love you all and I hope God has mercy on us and let's us drown in a hurry. They say it's the easiest way to die."

# Chapter 8

The bow of the barge rattled and shook like an earthquake as the huge rollers battered its steel frame. It wasn't our time. The platform never dropped and the lack of circulation in our throbbing arms and legs became secondary when once we were confident that we weren't going to be ditched in the ocean. Painful as they were, we took heart when we began to see faint lights on the shore a few miles ahead. At least we'd make it all the way to Wewak. In the inscrutable mind of the oriental, they had perhaps bound us so securely for fear of our jumping overboard in a suicidal escape. Lieutenant Asai might, in that event, be compelled to commit hari cari himself. He knew that Nip brass was expecting us in Wewak and that it was their prerogative to decide our fate-- non delivery might be fatal to him as well.

We were untied and hustled ashore onto a creaking pier with a dilapidated truck parked nearby. We mounted the truck, blind folded, and were transported through what seemed to be the edge of the town. For a short while we heard voices in that unpleasant language and the footsteps of many enemy soldiers, then quiet for a mile or so until we entered an area where at least a battalion of troops were quartered mostly in tents. With our blind folds removed, although it was dark, we saw a pleasant rolling valley, cleared of brush and comfortably accommodating the troops. Watanabi, who had been of little help to us, retired, leaving us under guards who permitted us to lie down on the grass with neither handcuffs nor any sort of physical restriction.

This second largest enemy bastion in the southwest Pacific by now held thousands of troops. Rabaul, to the north on New Britain was the largest. Here was the place that Tom Doyle, as well as the rest of us, hoped and believed would be our salvation with adequate food, medical attention and decent living quarters. We got no food, saw no medic and slept on the dewy grass.

The next morning at sun up we witnessed a curious ceremony by troops at rigid attention chanting a staccato oath or pledge of some sort--discordant but impressive. Four hundred voices chanting in unison and ardent devotion. I have never seen or heard anything among our own troops with a tenth as much dedication. Even the frantic "Heil Hitlers" of Nazi Germany that I had heard in newscasts were nowhere near as hypnotic. We were to witness this ceremony many times in the future and to learn that the ten minute recitation pledged the soldiers to fight for their Emperor and the glory of Japan against all odds and gladly to their death if necessary. It was recited in chilling sincerity.

Another breakfast of one rice ball and a cup of thin soup represented another disappointment.

A hundred yards from where we sat on the grass we noticed a detail of several men digging two wells, which seemed odd in that particular location. Down in the holes men would load a bucket of dirt which was hoisted to the top by rope when filled. They worked as though the project had to be finished in five minutes although its completion took several hours. The holes when finished were approximately 12 feet deep and 6 feet in diameter. Some well, we thought. Some prison we learned. Those holes were for us with four officers to live in one and four enlisted men in the other. Above ground barbed wire was strung around each hole, a completely superfluous precaution against escape by a barefoot allied aircrew in the middle of thousands of Japanese and with six hundred miles of jungle separating it from the nearest allied base.

"There's no way to figure these guys," said Martindale, "You know they can't put us down in those holes."

"They can't?" said Doyle. "How much?" They did. It was hot and it was cramped. An empty rice bucket was benevolently put in each hole substituting for a standard Hajoca facility. It was hard to believe but we believed. Twenty-one carat bastards was the mildest epithet we could label those twenty-one carat bastards.

These two holes in the ground were to be our home for seven days and nights. At meal time, which meant whenever someone felt disposed to feed us and was highly unpredictable, the standard rice ball and occasionally a small can of potato leaf soup, was lowered to us in a bucket. Every other day one prisoner was allowed to come up and carry the benjo bucket to a nearby garden where it was collected in steel drums and used as fertilizer. One advantage living underground offered was that we were protected from the sun except around noon time when the equatorial blaze was directly overhead and striking like a furnace. Another was that mosquitoes weren't so bad and those that descended became more or less trapped and we were able to kill them because they didn't have much flying space.

Our strength was ebbing, our beards were scruffy and unclean. Our spirits were low but at the end of a week a Japanese sergeant name Kato arrived from Rabaul and announced that he was a representative of the elite Kempe Tai or military police and that we were in his official custody. We hoped this meant we were now getting on a better track and it seemed that we were because Gunso Kato had us removed from the holes and taken to an area in the hills which was shady and much cooler. His insignia of rank was new and unfaded, his knee high boots were highly polished and he wore a flashy sword. On his left arm was a white arm band with splashy red Japanese characters identifying him as a member of the Kempe Tai, a rather impressive get-up topped off with a new gray green wool cap with a short visor and a bright red star above it. He also wore a cynical smile that fostered about as much trust as an Indian king cobra.

There was a large wooden building about a quarter of a mile from us that we could see through some trees standing on each side of a narrow dirt road leading to the building. I recognized this building as an alternate target I had attempted to bomb on several missions. Although I couldn't see the top of the building from the woods, I knew from experience that it bore a red cross on its roof but was not a hospital. It was the site of an anti-aircraft gun emplacement.

On one particular bombing mission out of Port Moresby I had a two star Air Force General as a co-pilot who wanted to look over the situation at Wewak. When my bomber was 10-12 miles from that same building with the red cross on top, just as I knew they would, the Jap gun emplacements opened up on us very ineffectively. My General co-pilot studied the site through binoculars but wouldn't allow me to fly any nearer. I assured him that the enemy gunners were inexperienced and presented little danger. He never the less, wouldn't allow me to fly any closer. I was considerably closer then and was hoping that I couldn't be identified as the pilot who had attacked the site several times with my regular co-pilot, Martindale. On the flight returning to Port Moresby, the General refused to secure his oxygen mask over his mouth and nose but intermittently took drafts from it and returned it to his lap. He gradually became a little giddy, a condition that was more dangerous than the flak at Wewak. Nearing home base a decision had to be made as to whether to cross the towering Owen-Stanley Mountains directly opposite Port Moresby or to proceed further south east which would take longer but afforded a much safer route at a lower altitude through a pass that was usually clear of thunder storms. I strongly opposed the former route but in his giddy state of mind through lack of oxygen, he insisted we push through the raging thunderstorm at 23,000 feet. When heavy icing conditions appeared in addition to violent turbulence the General twice attempted to take the controls and fly the ship, a job at which he was thoroughly incapable. I finally had to whack his wrists to restrain him and get us safely through. Unfortunately this was not a unique event. Many older pilots had excellent qualifications but very few at the top knew much about the new B-24 or its capabilities, or the vagaries of New Guinea weather which we younger pilots had learned the hard way.

Here at Wewak I now wondered if we would have the misfortune to encounter such lack of judgement in the Japanese brass.

It's a matter of opinion whether we did or did not, for on the second day on the hill it was announced that we would be interrogated that morning by high ranking officers. We were marched to a nearby spot where six luminaries were seated at tables. Several brief cases and mugs of tea adorned the tables. The scene was accentuated by a profusion of decorative ribbons and medals on the officers chests above their impressive swords. They had arrived at the spot by means of two staff cars the likes of which you could easily find in any second rate American junk yard.

As I was the pilot I was the first to be interrogated. Brought forward by the guards and required to kneel and bow deeply from the waist, I faced the commanding officer.

"Goot a morning," he addressed me in English, pleasantly enough.

"Ohayo goseimas," I replied in Japanese, equally as courteous. Then through the interpreter he said, "Oh, you speak Japanese? This interrogation will be much easier."

I explained that I only knew a few words which I suspected he already knew.

"Is there something we can do for you?" he asked condescendingly.

I have no idea what prompted my reply except to possibly create a spirit of camaraderie. "I would like a toothbrush, if possible," I answered.

The interpreter struggled to get this across whereupon the officer engaged in serious conversation with his staff followed by belly laughs all around and much refilling of their teacups.

A few guttural sounds of disgust ended that line of conversation.

"Where is the American Navy?" he asked incredulously.

"I haven't the least idea," I replied timidly.

"But you must know, you are an officer and a pilot."

"That doesn't qualify me to know such things."

"You must remember you are a prisoner and must cooperate with us or face consequences," he sternly threatened.

I asked for a pencil and paper and printed my name, rank and serial number and returned it to the commander adding that by International Law, that was all that was required of me.

They laughed again and spoke to the guards imperiously, who rushed up and kicked me into a prone position and lashed me a half dozen times with a bamboo rod. Then they set me back to my former position on knees handcuffed with my hands behind my back.

"You will now answer the question," he said.

"Well, if I must tell you, I saw an enormous concentration of

U.S. warships at Johnson Island when I passed there going to Australia several months ago," I lied. I hadn't been within hundreds of miles of Johnson Island. The officer seemed satisfied and the guards backed off.

So this is the game I thought. Then they wanted to know how many air dromes there were in Port Moresby. I lied again and answered six. A recent aerial photo of Moresby was shown me which clearly indicated my answer was wrong but it didn't seem to matter. More preposterous questions were asked and preposterous answers were given.

Each of my crew members went through a similar charade and the interrogation was halted on a note that puzzled us as to whether or not we had successfully duped our inquisitors. Their next move seemed to answer the puzzle as we were tied to the bumper of one of the staff cars with a rope around our waist but no restriction on our feet. Being drug over a rough road by a speeding automobile through various enemy encampments would provide royal entertainment for the troops and a most ignominious death for us--the height of oriental contempt.

The car began to move slowly and we followed at a walk. The deep ruts and pot holes made walking difficult especially for Martindale who was at the time suffering from more malarial attacks than the rest of us. He stumbled but quickly regained his feet and kept his individual rope from becoming taut. The speed increased gradually until we broke into a slow jog and then a trot. When it became necessary to actually run to prevent being jerked to the ground, the car stopped at our compound and we were untied and left with Gunso Kato and his Kempe Tai cadre.

Kato kept a very tight reign on us in this little camp. It was out of the main stream although we did have periodic visitors, mostly curiosity seekers of all types--some came merely to taunt us, others to practice their broken English but the majority only to stare inscrutably and leave in silence. Kato demanded that we, when approached by a soldier no matter what rank, bow at the waist and sit at attention. At first, this seemed so ingratiating that we resented it, but in most cases, the soldiers returned our courtesy.

Failure to observe this rule resulted in a dozen slaps across the face with a wide plastic ruler that Kato kept for this purpose. The same punishment came for our talking to each other when he had forbidden it. We were not tied up or restricted by any enclosure but required to sit on the ground at attention all day. Never knowing what to expect we nevertheless constantly believed that by being placed so near the make shift hospital, we would eventually be given some medical attention since we had lost a lot of weight and suffered from slight malarial attacks causing alternating chills and fever. We developed a painful itch and some of us had minor tropical yaws, a persistent unhealing sore around the ankle.

No medic appeared and after three or four days we gave up the idea when told we were moving again. A truck moved us down to the harbor on the fourth day and with very little fan fare or contact with troops. Kato, as a member of the Kempe Tai, didn't seem too popular with the troops, the reason being his self-imposed air of elitism, his swaggering sword and conspicuous arm band. We boarded a small civilian boat that barely accommodated the eight of us along with Kato and his three man squad. We were told we were going to an offshore island name Kariru.

"Oh my God, no!" I whispered to Sugden. "They know all about our friend Mot and his contact with Father Manion. This may be real bad for us and for Mot and Father Manion."

Kato shot an inquisitive eye at me and asked, "You know Kariru?" You bomb this island?"

The interpreter looked at me as though he thought I was lying and it unnerved me slightly. Better make it sound good I thought. These bastards are tricky, may know the whole story.

"There are German and American Missionaries on Kariru." Kato replied. "Just one American, I think."

"Oh, I'd like to speak to him. Do you think it's possible."

"Do you know him," Kato asked nonchalantly, as he squinted his eyes toward the approaching island.

I hoped the little anxiety sweat I was beginning to feel on my upper lip wasn't noticeable and replied with all the conviction I could muster, "Now, Gunso Dancho, how could that be possible. An Air Force Officer recently arrived in New Guinea and an American Missionary on a tiny island thousands of miles from the

United States?"

"Quite so," he replied evidently pleased that I had learned the word Dancho, a term of respect and authority which I attached to his title of sergeant. I breathed easier.

Rabaul Kempi Tai

# Chapter 9

A neat gravel path led up hill from the dock toward an area where several open air buildings stood more or less encircling a rather imposing structure built of a combination of stucco and wood giving evidence of its having been used a church or a school house. It had glass windows nicely framed and showing signs of having been painted a soft gray within recent years. This was the Mission Station we had heard about. As we passed one building we saw a tired old gas operated refrigerator. The familiar name of Kelvinator was like seeing an old friend. There was no electricity on the island. Several clean cut natives neatly dressed in lap laps stood around the building and gave only slight notice of the eight prisoners being marched to a camp adjoining this area.

We stopped at a small rectangular structure with a concrete floor and three sides. A drapery extended from one side out about six feet and hung from an overhead wire. The rest of the 100 square foot structure was open. Behind the not altogether closed curtain were shelves lined with books.

"This will be your nice home for a while," Kato said and then in no uncertain terms strongly admonished us to never, never go near or try to read the books behind the curtain. The warning almost inferred a death threat. The vista from our cement floor was pleasant. We looked down across a grove of trees that spread themselves almost to the water of a quiet bay. There were very few soldiers on the island but a considerable number of the most intelligent looking natives we had seen.

Kato made an effort to patronize the natives right away calling them up to explain who and what we were. The interpreter spoke Pidgin English as well but didn't realize that we also knew some basic Pidgin. He told them that we were enemies of Japan and also their enemy. The natives smiled ingratiatingly and at the same time gave us a feeling that the smiles were out of fear of the Gunso and an indication of sympathy for us.

The atmosphere became more relaxed on Kariru and from time to time we were told to work on several projects involving carpentry but mainly on digging air raid shelters. This work was also performed by the natives and often gave us the opportunity to talk to them secretly. We learned that they had all been formally employed by the Missionaries and that they were dumbfounded by the Japanese invasion and didn't understand the war at all. Some were converted to Catholicism and most were still loyal to their former masters. They had attended school taught by Catholic Brothers and Sisters and looked after medically by trained personnel.

That was all gone now for the whole Catholic contingent was incarcerated elsewhere on the island and treated shabbily--yes, the natives knew Father Manion and thought the world of him and prayed regularly for him. We saw very few of the Missionaries and were told that 42 of them including Father Manion, a native girl and two Chinese children were taken aboard a Japanese destroyer sometime earlier and were shipped to Rabaul. In 1946 I learned that these unfortunate people constituted the victims of the "Akihaze Massacre" which was documented in a work by Rev. Ralph Wiltgen S.V.D. titled "The History of the Catholic Church in Northeast New Guinea." All 42 of them en route to Rabaul were taken to the stern of the Akihaze individually and machine gunned and allowed to fall backwards into the sea.

The various labor projects we performed involved moving about on the island to some extent. One project involved digging a well from which location we were able to observe the construction of a sea plane base by the Japs. We also saw a few of the Missionaries from time to time at a distance but were not allowed to communicate with them. They had been lucky enough not to have been shipped out on the Akihaze, however all but two were later shipped to Hollandia safely and liberated by the American army when it captured Hollandia. The two that remained on Kariru, Fathers May and Reif, were subsequently beheaded because they knew about the beheading of four American flyers at nearby Bargaram. Father Andrew Gerstner, who had seen the eight of us on Kariru, gave me this information in a letter from Wewak in 1948. He also gave me the sad information that our great benefactor Mot and his son Lamouche were drowned at sea in a violent storm. He further informed me that several days after the eight of us departed Wageo Island, Japanese soldiers arrived having been informed of our presence there. Mot had denied everything, gave them two chickens and they departed satisfied with their loot after a perfunctory search of the island. (See Epilogue)

A Korean laborer soon arrived at our place under heavy guard. Otaka, for whatever crime he had committed, had been severely beaten prior to his arrival, but no matter, his cruel punishment continued for days. He was tied to one of the heavy posts supporting our roof and slept on the concrete floor just as we did. Through either ignorance or despair one night he managed to escape. It was absurd to think he would not be recaptured as he had no way to leave the island and of course, he was recaptured two days later and returned to our place. His previous torture was mild by comparison to what he then received. He was made to sit on his knees on the concrete morning, noon and most of the night while the guard beat him with clubs for hours. They burned him with their cigarettes. When he fell asleep and topped over they hung weights on his back suspended from a string on his forehead preventing him from toppling over.

We never knew his crime other than his effort to escape. After a week of this, his punishment subsided and he more or less became a member of our crew. He spoke a little broken English and told us he was fortunate to be alive. We agreed.

After a month on Kariru, eating mostly the burnt crust of rice that was boiled in empty ammunition cans and scraped from the bottom in layers, Kato told us we were to be shipped to Rabaul, New Britain. No preparations were necessary as we had no possessions beyond the tattered clothes on our backs. We were shoeless, gaunt, unhealthy and thoroughly exhausted from the work in the sun without protection; but most of all from the lack of food. The suggestion of a three or four hundred mile trip at sea to Rabaul sounded like real relief. Rabaul was the largest enemy stronghold in the South Pacific. It was highly possible that there was an organized Prisoner of War Camp there regulated by the humane rules of International Law.

**90th Bombardment Group (Heavy)**
**321st Squadron – My Outfit**

# Chapter 10

A Japanese sub-chaser tied up in the harbor for no more than forty-five minutes while we boarded. Allied bombers had frequently visited nearby Wewak in recent days and the Navy boys didn't want to be caught moored in the harbor.

We got under way promptly and relished the fresh ocean air in our faces since we were tied up on the forward steel deck of the sub-chaser. I reckoned it cruised at around 18-20 knots with its quiet diesel turbines. Kato and his squad lounged near us most of the trip. There was a certain animosity between the Jap Army and Navy that was clearly discernable. Since we were not their direct responsibility the sailors were friendly to us much to Kato's disapproval. They practiced their English on us while offering cigarettes. They smoked a different brand from the Army issue. Engel complimented them on the quality of their brand and joked around with them amicably. He ingratiated himself to an extent that the sailors offered us a few salted crackers with a hint of butter on them. They were absolutely beautiful and so appreciated, all to the dire consternation of a sullen Kato Gunso.

About half way to Rabaul the ship docked at Manus Island at a port named Loregau as evening approached. There was a large military detachment stationed there. We had previously bombed the place back in December '42 and were glad to see it from ship board however little could be seen.

We spent most of the night on the steel deck while Naval Officers conducted whatever business was necessary. Several hours before dawn we set sail again for the last leg of the cruise to Rabaul and arrived at mid-morning.

The giant Simpson harbor in Blanche Bay was teeming with activity. It is one of the deepest water harbors in the world as it is surrounded by several semi-active volcanoes, the two most prominent of which are called the Mother and the Daughter. Wisps of smoke and steam rise from them almost continuously. The town of Rabaul with a prewar population of perhaps 800 Occidentals, three or four hundred Chinese and a varying number of natives and half castes, stretched along the waterfront for a couple of miles at the north-eastern portion of a huge horseshoe shaped bay. Freighters, transports, small barges and huge naval vessels were anchored along the wharfs and out in the bay, all remarkably reflecting on Oriental design.

Kato hustled us into a waiting truck anxious to again be in full charge after our comparative freedom on the sub-chaser. We drove to the center of the little town and unloaded at Kempe Tai Headquarters, an old wooden building, the front of which had formerly been a Chinese Tailer's shop. There were three rooms in the rear of the shop and a small open court yard facing the rooms. The headquarters in front was manned by several non-commissioned officers, all friends of Kato, all similarly disposed toward POW's.

Before being shown to our quarters, we stood at attention in the office while Kato recounted his trip down to Wewak with this buddies listening intently. We could understand snatches of his story particularly when he accented it with gestures of ridicule of us and bravado on his part. He ended the account in an emotional tirade about our association with the sailors on the sub-chaser. Now buoyed by the presence of his friends and their complicity, his rage overwhelmed him and he stalked in front of us with his plastic ruler and slapped each of us across the face many times until finally reaching Engel.  Here he stopped for a moment and delivered a personalized blast of sound and fury before attacking him with full strength. The slight favors Engel had received from the sailors was paid for dearly.

A new interpreter appeared and for thirty minutes we were lectured on the political guilt of the U.S. and England and the aspirations and sure success of Japan. We were asked questions but an attempt to answer was met with a slap from Kato. He ended with a note of proud dignity saying that in spite of our guilt we would be treated well.  Japanese Bushido demanded it much in contrast to American policy which invariably required the beheading of enemy prisoners. My protest of this statement brought Kato back into action at the end of which we were shown to our cell.

"What's all that Bushido shit?" said Wynne as he looked around the tiny dark rom.  "If this is their idea of treating us well, I'd as soon go back to a black Mississippi convict camp which would look like the Senator Hotel in Sacramento compared to this place." All of us had had some high times in the old Senator Hotel just before leaving the States.  Management never knew it but that fine old hotel came very close to destruction one night in September '42 by reason of an orgy of cigarettes and whiskey and wild, wild women involving a certain air crew of the 90th Bomb Group.
 "What's that square hole in the wall for?"
"That's for room service, you dummy," said Farnell.  "That's where our quail on toast will be served from the outside."

The door and walls to the cell were made of heavy timber, the floor was rough unfinished lumber with half inch gaps between the boards.  The only light came through the upper portion of the front wall where eight two by fours spaced six inches apart, support the corrugated tin roof.  The metal had been salvaged from somewhere and showed many nail holes.  Tiny streams of light beamed through them at various angels.  We knew that rain would do the same.  So would allied bombs and bullets.  We were still wearing the remains of our uniforms which in some cases meant G.I. underwear.  The Japs offered us no clothing nor did they issue us a blanket or even a straw mat to sleep on.  The last meal had been breakfast on the sub-chaser and it wasn't until just before dark that food arrived.  The door to the small square hole in the front wall was pushed open by an anonymous guard and eight balls of rice were presented by the bare hands of the guard.  Also included was three small perch size pieces of fish which surprised us.  It was also surprised us when we smelled it.  Rotten fish had to be a cruel joke and we told the guard that was our impression.  He was infuriated that we condemned his offering and even threatened to take back the rice which we by now had learned to love and ravenously looked forward to.  O.K. our fantasy was over.  Rabaul was no different except that it certainly had to have an abundance of food to support the vast army and navy stationed there.  We just weren't included on their hospitality list.  Try to get used to it, we said.

Days drug into weeks and the brightest day of the week was Sunday.  On Sunday nights the ball of rice and sometimes can of potato leaf soup, was replaced by a small mesh bag of hard tack. There were twelve or fourteen tiny hard biscuits and a couple of marble size lumps of vari-colored sugar. These highly prized biscuits began to cause a serious problem among us about the second time we received them. To break the monotony of sitting around the walls all day, we started gambling with them. Each man would ante a biscuit into the middle of the floor followed by guessing games created by a non-gambling member. The guy giving the correct answer won seven biscuits. The questions then passed to the next non-participant, and a greedy new winner took the prize. Treachery soon arose. The questioner had wide discretion over the correct answer and favoritism crept into the game. Accusations were made and often followed by pitifully weak fist fights. The guards were aware of what was happening, but made no effort to stop it. In fact, they encouraged it and it was their delight in our antagonism to each other that brought us to our senses and we discontinued the games.

Otaka, the Korean laborer sat in the cell with us for several weeks without further beatings. He became a good friend and gave us a little insight into the ways of the Oriental mind. Eventually he was taken out, more or less as a trusty, and assigned to a work detail. We were sorry to see him go and hoped we would see him again, because from his being on the outside, he might somehow provide us with valuable information.

Our gambling with biscuits was replaced by story telling, recounting old movies, word games and constant conversation; anything to keep our minds off hunger. This activity wasn't allowed by the all the guards but some permitted it and standing just outside the cell would try to understand what we were saying. Some had studied a little English in school and were very curious. They too were terribly bored by long hours of duty sitting or standing outside our cell. Three or four guards rotated every eight hours. Most were stoic but some tried to communicate. We learned their names and their rank. We learned to say good morning, thank you, I'm hungry, sick or in pain, are you married, how old are you and the names of the days of the week and the months.

We also learned that there were two other American prisoners living in an adjoining building and it was good to hear that they would soon be joining our group. Ray Berry, a T.B.F. pilot and his rear gunner, Cyphus Kelly, made us shutter when they were brought into the cell. They looked so emaciated. Of course, their reaction to us was the same. We were accustomed to each others's gaunt faces, but the face of a newcomer in this condition was shocking.

Berry and Kelly were both from the Chicago area and had been in combat about as long as we had. They had been shot down considerably after us but were captured immediately and brought to Rabaul a month before we arrived. Kelly was only 18 years old and a walking skeleton. He couldn't have weighed a hundred pounds and he was about 5 feet 10 inches tall. Small sores literally covered his body. There was hardly a square inch of flesh without a sore, all very visible to us as he wore a fundoshi, the Japanese name for a lint cloth. Joining us helped his spirit but did little for ours at the first sight of him. Ray Berry was getting along about like the rest of us having lost probably no more than 20-30 pounds.

Two new story tellers was a relief. Berry's pride in the size and quality of his home town Chicago challenged Tom Doyle's reverence for Kansas City, his hometown. Their life's story was pleasant to hear after listening to our own for so long and so many times.

As we all began to break out in sores in various degrees we kiddingly accused Kelly of being contagious-not much of a joke. Lack of vitamins was the real culprit and sores were manifestations of scurvy and beri-beri.

One day a non-descript Japanese appeared at our window and asked in fairly good English if any of us understood radar. Along with his briefcase he had a piece of radio equipment evidently salvaged from a downed American airplane. Sensing that he connected the salvage with radar, I offered full knowledge and was invited out of the cell and into the Kempe Tai front offices where we conversed.

My assumption was correct, he believed the radio equipment

was a radar receiver so I was on fairly safe ground. Our B-24's didn't have radar and I'd only read a smattering of what it was and how it worked. I was immediately offered a cigarette as inducement to really open up on a technical subject. I successfully confounded him with a mixture of electric and science fiction jargon long forgotten from high school physics and Tom Swift stories. I drew it out for over an hour and smoked half his cigarettes. Toward the end he asked some question that he was particularly anxious to have answered. I pretended to know the answer but gave him the impression that it would be too traitorous of me to reveal it; whereupon he produced from his briefcase a lovely chocolate bar, believing correctly that I would answer.

It was a bad mistake for me to recount all of this to my buddies upon returning to the cell. Giving spurious information to the enemy became very popular and there was never a lack of volunteers after that episode.

Home Base – Jackson Strip
Near Port Moresby, November, 1942.

# Chapter 11

Sometime in early June 1943, about five months after our hitting the drink off Wewak, an allied plane was shot down near Rabaul and the one surviving crew member was captured. Second Lieutenant Jack King Wisener, the bombardier of a B-17 belonging to the 43rd Bomb Group and of Port Moresby, was brought into our prison. Jack was from Wells, Texas and the epitome of the popular conception of Texans. A good looking guy, over six feet tall and well over 200 lbs. His interrogation lasted only a few days, after which he was put in the cell with us. We were sorry about his misfortune, but what a joy to have some up-to-date news of the war! Especially good news since we had been indoctrinated daily by the Japs about their victories everywhere in the Pacific. They even told us they had bombed the U.S. west coast. Their version of this bombing was far form the truth, although we did learn later that the enemy had launched hundreds of tiny air balloons with a small grenade attached which had floated across the Pacific and a dozen or so actually were reported being found in the mountains of Washington state. We doubted their stories but had no way of knowing what to believe. The Jap forces certainly had been on the offensive when we were shot down and here at Rabaul five months later their apparent strength and cocky attitude gave us some reason to believe they might actually be invading Australia as they said.

Jack Wisener blew all of that into a cocked hat. He told us that in March our air force had intercepted a Jap convoy coming down the northwest side of New Britain headed for Lae on New Guinea. The convoy consisted of seven or eight destroyers and ten or twelve transport and cargo ships. Their mission was to reinforce Lae. The Jap ground forces had been defeated at Buna further south and had retreated overland to Lae. We knew none of this. Our bombers, as few as were available, kept the convoy under constant attack with mild results until it reached the Vitiaz Straits which separates New Britain and New Guinea at which point our B-25's, A-20's, P-47's, P-38's and the Australian Braufighters could reach it. The battle lasted three days and resulted in a tremendous allied victory. Jack told us that early in the battle one of the Jap destroyers had rescued several hundred survivors of a sinking Jap transport and had managed to rush them on into Lae. Other than that, the rest of the convoy was either sunk by our planes or retreated back to Rabaul. Of the estimated 7,000 troops in the transports, nearly 4,000 were killed or drowned. Jack said giant sharks were seen attacking the dead of dying troops and that the surrounding water was a sea of blood. Several of the destroyers had been sunk and the rest badly battered. Nothing short of a full course meal could have suited us better than this news. We wondered how many such victories would it take to win this war, but one thing we knew for certain--allied air power could annihilate surface vessels--a Midway rerun. Our guard's occasional reference to beheading by now seemed a little less likely giving us reason to place our hope for salvation in survival until the end of the war.

It didn't take long however, for Jack's healthy two hundred pounds to deteriorate and his spirit went with it. The first few weeks of imprisonment with three tiny rice balls a day was as crucial to the mind as to the body. Long periods of stony silence and indifference to the rest of the group worried us when we took the time to forget our own condition. On a difficulty scale of a hundred, giving up cigarettes is a one and giving up food is a flat one-hundred. My crew and Berry and Kelly were somewhat acclimated to the reality of prison conditions, but Jack was in the torturous adjustment period; if in fact adjustment was possible.

A welcomed diversion from monotony occurred one night in early July 1943 when sleep seemed impossible. We heard activity in the Kempe Tai front office followed by the arrival of someone in the cell adjoining ours. The Japs were serious about Shoto, or lights out after dark, and although we never had any lights, they did have carbide lanterns but seldom used them. The night was unusually dark and it was impossible to see what was going on. Muffled voices followed by dead silences. I moved quietly from my usual sleeping place on the pine board floor and sat up against the common wall between the two cells and listened for any sound or clue that might tell me who or what the newcomer was. I could only hear labored breathing and a few groans. I continued to listen but was afraid to speak. After a while I heard someone faintly whistling a few bars of "Summertime" from "Porgy and Bess." The whistler had no idea where he was nor that we were in the next cell. When he broke off, I picked up the tune, just loud enough not to be heard by the guards outside. When I ended a bar the whistler picked it up again. There was no doubt about it, a new American was next door.

The next morning after Meshi, the new prisoner was taken to the front office for interrogation. As he passed our cell we saw the pitiful figure of a guy struggling to walk with his head bent over nearly to his knees. He cut his eyes in our direction and we returned a compassionate smile and a thumbs up signal. Any other greeting was unthinkable.

This route continued for about two weeks when finally his interrogation ended and Joe Holguin was allowed to join us in the front cell. No other word described Joe better than spunky. He was the sole survivor of a B-17 that was shot down at night and crashed in the mountains some 50 miles from Rabaul. Joe parachuted from the burning plane only a couple of minutes before it crashed. He unfortunately floated over the raging fire which burned his chute enough to accelerate his fall tremendously. He landed in the branches of a tree which variously broke his back, punctured his chin to the base of his tongue and mangled his left knee. He hung in the tree all night not knowing until daylight that he was suspended not more than a few feet from the ground. He cut his shroud lines and fell painfully to the ground. Crawling on his stomach he found a couple of straight sticks which he used as crutches to propel himself half prone for several miles the first day. The second day he found a river and floated on a log downstream hoping to reach the coast and possible rescue but was intercepted by natives who seemed friendly enough. They carried him to a small village and placed him on a mat inside a straw hut giving him coconut milk and papaya. During his four days there one native told him that he would be betrayed by certain natives that had turned pro Japanese. The loyal natives were powerless to prevent it, being fearful of their own lives. On the fifth day a patrol arrived and Joe being semi-conscious only remembered that the officer in charge bent over him with a pistol in hand. He, like all of us, felt that his time had come until the officer offered him a lighted cigarette and prepared to carry him back to their camp.

Not long after Joe arrived, a Marine F.4.U. pilot named
Charlie Lanphier was brought in. Friendships developed unusually
fast in prison, and I quickly learned to love Joe and Charlie. Both
were Catholic as was Tom Doyle and to their everlasting credit,
they taught the rest of us to say the Rosary from which we derived
a lot of comfort.

**Japanese coastal shipping under low level attack.**

# Chapter 12

During the late summer and fall of 1943 the Allies had taken the offensive in a big way. Lae had been secured in New Guinea by ground forces, and advanced air fields were built at spots along the coast allowing shorter range aircraft to attack Jap installations at Finshafen, Saidor, Aleishafen, Boram, Wewak and But on the north coast of New Guinea, as well as Cape Gloucester, Arawe, Gasmata, Talasea and Rabaul on New Britain. Heavy bombers were even enjoying the luxury of fighter escorts to some targets. Fire power was increased on attack planes, B-24's now had nose turrets, and more maneuverable fighter planes came on the scene that were as capable, or perhaps more capable than the Jap Zero. These improvements led to the stunning victories for the Allies but not without losses. Army, Navy, Marine and Australian aircraft personnel were shot down and captured around targets all along the front. From August, 1943 through January, 1944, new prisoners came streaming into our compound. The thirteen of us commiserated with the newcomers: Maj. Cox, Cpl. Griffin, Lt. Joe Nason, Lt. Al Quinones, Sgt. Esco Palmer, Lt. James Warren, Lt. Robert Sherman, Lt. Tom Fessigner, Sgt. John Giles, Lt. William Hanks, Lt. John Fitzgerald, Lt. Harold Tuck, Lt. James Miller, Lt. Donald Evans, Lt. Stookey, Maj. Ralph Celli, Sgt. John Barron, Sgt. William Harris, Sgt. Mike Kicera, Ken Kershner, Lt. Joe Hill, Lt. Andy Borders, Lt. Walter Mayberry, Lt. Barthoff, Lt. Brendoz, Sgt. Ronnie Ull, Sgt. McLeaf, Lt. Kuhn, Maj. Kobig, Ens. John Osborn, Lt. Clements, Ens. Art Teal, Ens. Bill Wells, Lt. Donald Atkiss and Sgt. Dick Lannigan. Australian and New Zealand personnel were also captured and brought in from time to time some among them having been with "Ferdinand," the coast watchers, such as John Murphy, Bob Cassidy and Lt. Bedkober. Jack Fenwick was a survivor of an Australian Catalina which crashed into a mountain in Bouganville. A Major Todd and Lt. Vickers were with the RAAF and RNZAR respectively; neither of whom had any respect for the air-cooled engines of their P-40's. Others were brought in later so that the number of prisoners gradually increased to 78 at one time or another. The three adjoining cells were grossly inadequate for everyone to stretch out at night without being entangled with his neighbor. Everyone quickly came down with a combination of malaria, beri-beri, yaws and/or scurvy. Lack of protein or vitamins brought on serious cases of edema: an abnormal accumulation of serous fluid causing swelling in all parts of the body.

On November 13, 1943, an extremely lucky group of eight Americans and one Australian was arbitrarily called out of the cell and without any fanfare was put on a naval vessel and shipped to Japan. The group included Maj. Cox of Knoxville, Tenn.; Lt. Robert Martindale, my co-pilot of Brownsville, Texas; Lt. Jack Wisener of Wells, Texas; Sgt. Leslie Burnett, my engineer of Rocky Mount, NC; Sgt. Fred Engel, my radio operator of Chicago, Il; PFC Cephus Kelly of Chicago; Cpl. Griffin of Texas; Sgt. Frank Wynn of Marigold, Miss., my tail gunner; and Bob Cassidy, an Australian. They reached Japan safely after an arduous trip at sea. This was confirmed after the war but at the time we really never knew if the Japs were telling the truth about their arrival. There was no rhyme or reason for their selection as evacuees that we could ever determine. From that date forward it would have been an extremely hazardous trip as our submarines were operating in force and through our old friend Otaka, the Korean, we learned that the only supplies coming out of Japan to Rabaul arrived by cargo submarines mostly at night. The remainder of us had mixed emotions over our prospects of also being evacuated to Japan. While conditions there could hardly have been worse than at Rabaul, we imagined the home-land would be quite an improvement. On the other hand, the long voyage in the hole of a Japanese ship through U.S. Naval infested waters was a dismal prospect.

In mid summer 1943 when our ranks were relatively small, we were privileged to come out of the cell and work. Never on any of these occasions were more than half our group physically able to work, but those who felt they could endure it were eager to get the fresh air and a promised reward of food. The food never arrived, but we did get a few cigarettes. The work consisted of carrying coconut logs suspended by rope from bamboo poles and positioned around the walls of bomb shelters which we had previously dug. The top of the shelters were covered with huge logs 18 to 20 inches in diameter. We removed the dirt from the pits in burlap bags similarly suspended from poles and carried away on the shoulders of a two-man team. The work was supervised by the guards and when completed made a formidable shelter, but we were not allowed to enter them during air raids.  We were allowed, however, to dig a small cave through the back wall of our cell which provided some small protection from bombs, but was used mostly as a hiding place to smoke cigarette butts that we were able to pick up off the ground or steal from a guard's pack.  Several times we stole bits of food from the guard's ration and upon returning to the cell would eat it in the shelter of the little cave.  The penalty for being caught at this was unimaginable.  It was a desperate act but highly tempting.

An old horse blanket had been given as a present to Joe Nason who was pitifully sick at the time.  We unraveled a long thread from the blanket and hung it in our cave.  One of us was able to sneak a lighted cigarette into the cell and we lit the end of the blanket thread.  It would smolder for days before being replaced by another thread when burned out.  If, during an air raid with the guards down in their shelter, someone had a cigarette butt or two, by blowing furiously on the smoldering end of the thread, he could light his cigarette.  After a particularly harrowing allied raid which shook the foundation of every structure in Rabaul, the guards eventually came back to their post to find a cloud of smoke, but the guards were surprised to find us uninjured and never identified the smoke as coming from tobacco.

On the whole that summer there had been relatively few air raids which was the reason a few of us were allowed to work outside on the bomb shelters.  Our guards ridiculed the inactivity of the allied forces and declared that the war would soon be over since the Americans had given out of steam.  It was easy to believe.  One day, however, while working outside we noticed a lone American P-38 flying over Rabaul at what I'm sure was it's maximum altitude, 35 or 40 thousand feet making no threatening gestures.  The guard laughed and said the pilot was afraid to come any closer.  We, however, recognized the flight as a photo reconnaissance mission, which foretold a welcomed offensive.  We were correct.  The outside work continued for a few days with the workers getting no extra food and the non-workers getting less.  The Jap theory was "no work, no food."

Around September 1943 the B-24's and B-17's went back into action in a big way by bombing Rabaul Harbor and the air fields constantly. The little town itself was not of strategic importance and therefore not a direct target. Nevertheless, many a stray bomb came our way because we were only a mile from the harbor and a certain air field not much further away. We counted up to nearly a thousand bombings before we quite counting. We became so accustomed to raids that we were able to listen to bombers engines, calculate their direction and callously decline rushing into our cave. On many daylight raids we actually saw the stick of bombs falling through the air causing a unique swooshing sound followed by thunderous explosions. When pattern bombing was employed by a flight of six or eight heavies dropping one thousand pound bombs, the detonation was of such high frequency that the usual sound could hardly be heard. Instead we simply felt the ear drum ringing from heat and concussion.

The allied offensive was taking place on a broad front as evidenced by new prisoners being brought in from places like Wewak and Bougainville. The day of my unfortunate mission to Wewak, January 20th, marked the beginning of a huge concentration of enemy troops and air power in that area. One such prisoner was an outstanding pilot of a B-25 named Maj. Ralph Chelli. Ralph said he had led a squadron of 25's on a strafing attack against Dagua air drome on the morning of August 18th. The nearby Japanese air fields at Wewak and Boram had been completely surprised by our heavies, followed by strafing B-25's the previous day. Jap aircraft had been lined up wing to wing along the runways and tremendous Jap losses resulted. When Chelli led his flight into Dagua the following day, the anti-aircraft batteries were ready and Jap fighters were in the air. He nevertheless shot up a row of enemy planes on the ground while his own plane burst into flames. Chelli called his wingman and told him to take over the command of the flight, then he crashed into the sea. He was captured and joined us in Rabaul several weeks later in foul shape but in good spirits.

One of the most interesting prisoners brought to Rabaul during my nearly three years tenure was Capt. John J. Murphy. Murph had been an Australian Patrol Officer in New Guinea before the war and his intimate knowledge of the territory and native affairs qualified him immediately for a position with "Ferdinand" as a coast watcher.

Of all the continuously hazardous duty in the Pacific War, coast watching deserves a place at the top. This volunteer group of intrepid Australians camped under the noses of the Japanese throughout the war and radioed valuable intelligence information back to the allies. They rescued American airmen from enemy-held islands surrounded by enemy dominated seas. They saved the lives of numerous missionaries and displaced natives trapped behind enemy lines. The secrecy of their organization was maintained from dimly lit jungle camps, hidden tree top lookouts and hostile beaches. Its members are credited with some of the most amazing jungle treks of the war and their contribution to the ultimate victory in the South Pacific has been described as completely invaluable.

On September 28, 1943 the U.S. submarine Grouper surfaced off Cape Orford high on the south coast of New Britain with 16 coast watchers aboard. A coast watcher already stationed on this enemy-held coast signaled the Grouper to disembark its passengers, and that the landing site was temporarily clear of Japanese. They took to their rubber boats in high seas in total darkness and successfully made the landing. Murph's objective was to travel down the coast and set up a post near Gasmata, some one-hundred and forty miles to the southwest. A major portion majority of the interior of New Britain, like New Guinea, consists of towering mountains, criss-crossed with ridges, steep gullies and nearly impenetrable jungle growth. That being so, the Japs made little attempt to control the interior or its wild mountain tribes. The coastal trek bore nearly all the traffic. Murph was accompanied by another party of coastal watchers half way to Gasmata, at which point the accompanying party set off to the north where friendly natives, the Nakanai people, assisted them quickly to their post on the north coast east of Talasea. "Ferdinands" plans required that the several different parties reach their post by November 1st. Murph now had only 14 days to reach is post seventy miles away. Had he been given more time he could have traveled through the jungles and avoided the coastal trek which was well combed by Jap patrols. He and his party, consisting of a radio operator, an Australian soldier and eight natives, decided to risk the coast road in the interest of time. They made their way uneventfully for several days until a disloyal native reported the party's presence to a large Jap patrol which engaged them and killed several of Murphy's carriers. Murph and the rest scurried into the jungle and were comparatively safe until other natives again betrayed them. A short fire fight killed his radio man and the soldier and captured Murph. They interrogated him constantly before and after he arrived at our prison, and at one point he was made to dig his own grave to be used if he didn't cooperate and reveal the location of the other coast watchers that landed with his party. Somehow he satisfied his interrogators much as I had done at Wewak and his would-be grave became an overgrown jungle pit that barely missed its intended function.

After joining us in our cell Murph became a valuable addition as he spoke perfect Pidgin English. As a matter of fact, he had written a pidgin English dictionary that was distributed to the allied forces all over the area. Native prisoners were often put in the cell with us and at these times Murph learned a lot from them about the goings-on around Rabaul. He had even previously known some of the natives that were now doing forced labor for the Kempe Tai.

In November after the eight Americans and one Australian had been shipped out to Japan there was still twenty or thirty prisoners left using two of the three cells. Luckily, Murph was in my cell. "Meals" were being served by various natives who would bring up a bucket of rice, shape it into balls by hand and pass it in through the one square foot window where it was received by a prisoner appointed to receive it. Murph was everyone's choice to do the receiving since he could communicate perfectly with the native to the exclusion of the guard standing by.

For a period of over six or seven weeks a young half-caste named Benny Yamasta was serving us. Murph had known him before the war and identified him to us an illegitimate son of Errol Flynn, the movie actor, who had also lived in Rabaul pre-war. Benny was scared of the Japs but what worried him most was the idea of an American invasion. He constantly sought advice from Murph while he was serving the rice balls. If there were twenty prisoners in the cell, and the number was changing every few days, Murphy confused him on the count almost consistently. Having passed in, say eight balls, Benny would ask something like, "When should I expect the Americans to invade?"

Murphy would answer while receiving ball number nine, then ten, then eleven, "Benny, old friend, it's hard to tell but certainly by Christmas time."

"What should I do when they come?" Benny would ask.

"Wear anything white, if you can find it, and stay as close to the native women as you can." Murph would then pick up the ball count back at eight while receiving more.

"Then how do I reach the Americans and what do I say to them," Benny would ask.

By the time Murph's drawn out explanation was finished and several more balls taken in, Murph's ball count was only up to eleven so that at many meals Murph had suckered our nervous and inquisitive rice boy out of three or four extra balls. The extras were distributed fairly and on a rotational basis so that in a week's time almost every prisoner got at least one extra tennis ball size lump of white rice. This was a tremendous boost to morale, particularly to those who had been there long enough to adjust to the diet.

Almost invariably when a new prisoner was brought in, he would refuse to eat this rice ball for several days due to injury, sickness or shock and, of course, he had not long been away from full course meals. This induced the old timers to try to entice the new guy to sit by him, knowing he would voluntarily forfeit his rice for a few days and the lucky recipient was usually the guy next to him. I point to this with no pride but in our defense I must say we made a half-hearted attempt to convince him that he should eat. After a short period, the new guy usually adjusted and became an old timer hoping the next new prisoner would sit by him.

Sadly not everyone adjusted. Mental attitude was the criteria for survival. Uniquely, the biggest, healthiest guys often were the first to decline. Walter Mayberry, an all-southern football player from Florida went from a 220-pound former athlete down to about 150 pounds in practically no time. The coast watcher, Lt. Bedkober, stood at least six feet four inches and was a picture of health, although dejected when he came in. He had spent months in jungle training before being captured and was not the kind of guy you'd want to tangle with in a brawl. He was a thoroughly honorable guy with deep devotion to duty as the circumstances of his capture reveals.

Before taking his assigned post on Bougainville, Bedkober was put in charge of several Australian airmen who had been rescued from a crashed Catalina deep in enemy territory. The airmen were injured and unable to move about in the jungle very well. Bedkober's small party hoped to hide the airmen long enough from them to recuperate sufficiently to travel. The party was surprised by a Jap patrol and although Bedkober could easily have slipped away into the bush, he stayed until out of ammunition, then threw his weapon down and walked toward the enemy. Only he and the injured Jack Fenwick survived the fight and both were taken prisoner.

In Rabaul, Bedkober became morose from the first day. He refused to eat. For the first time and for what unknown reason, the guards showed some compassion for a prisoner. After no more than a couple of weeks Bedkober's condition seemed critical and one of the guards brought a few bananas to the cell especially for him. In no uncertain terms but fortunately in English, Bedkober told the guard to stick the bananas in his nose. In world record time the rest of us intervened and explained that Bedkober had thanked the guard, thanked the Japanese army and long live the Emperor for the bananas. Bedkober was too far gone to again state his case. We didn't eat the peeling but used them to salve our sores. The next morning Bedkober couldn't be aroused. He was dead.

At this time I believe there were three adjoining cells being used but with no connection between them except a common wall. Within minutes of the discovery of Bedkober's death the chilling news passed from cell to cell. Not one of us was without injury or disease of some sort and all with pretty dismal prospects, yet Bedkober's death came as a shock. I don't know why but the fantasy of survival had been so strong even under bleak circumstances that his death, our first in prison, crushed our spirits. No one mentioned it aloud but this reality focused one thought in our minds--who's next? It was enigmatic that Bedkober's death struck us so gravely when we had all had buddies dying in combat or by some accident or even in a military hospital. Those cases had not been nearly so traumatic. The fear and anxiety came from the mere fact that nothing was done to save his life and that we could expect the same indifference.

The swollen faces, the puffy thighs and ankles, even bloated scrotums was a gruesome sight but painless. The many sores on hands and legs however was another matter. The terrible itching they brought on could only be helped by scratching but this broke the skin still further and caused more oozing of a clear fluid that at times puddled on the floor. Scratching for relief with fingernails or a broom straw was intolerable. A wet path would follow the straw. The closest thing to relief came from a wadded up piece of paper rolled around on the surface, if you could find paper. Paper was at a premium, however, on account of its constant use at the Benjo bucket due to rampant dysentery. The accompanying chills from malaria made fleshless bones rattle on the floor like a hound dog scratching fleas.

More deaths followed. Art Teal and Bill Wells were taken from prison by Jap navy personnel in December, blindfolded, handcuffed and led away never to be heard from again. The only example of Bushido of any benefit to us came about after a prisoner died. We were asked what type of ceremony, if any, was customary for the dead. We told them that, in addition to saying prayers and recounting the goodness of the deceased, food should be placed at his head, to which the Japs complied and added an incense punk at his feet. This, we said, was properly done while smoking and reflecting on life's tribulations. These somewhat callous suggestions netted us a bowl of rice or sometimes a few bananas to be shared and a few cigarettes after which natives came in and wrapped the body in old rice bags and carried it away to where we never knew.

The strongest prisoner was selected daily to empty the Benjo bucket. It required considerable strength to carry the bucket from our cell to a nearby garden. One prisoner made a near fatal mistake when he slipped while carrying the bucket and spilled some of its contents. He received a bashing that eventually resulted in the loss of an eye. Carrying the Benjo bucket could be injurious to your health yet getting out into the open air and away from the stench of the cell was often worth it, particularly if a half-way decent guard accompanied you and let you rest a few seconds with half a cigarette. It was also refreshing to see cucumbers and other vegetables rising verdantly out of the red volcanic ash showing signs of renewed life in the middle of so much death and destruction.

Cruelty seemed so much a part of the Japanese nature as it was not only inflicted on us but on the natives and sometimes on their own people. The Korean Otaka seemed to accept it as a way of life, being Oriental, but neither we nor the native recipients found it at all credulous. Many nights were made sleepless by the continuous howling and moaning of native prisoners being beaten for some petty crime after which they were thrown into a cell with us with a mass of bloody whelps that took weeks to heal.

**90th Bombardment Group (Heavy)**
**Official Insignia**

# Chapter 13

Across the dirt street in front of our prison was a large two story wooden structure that our guards called the Comfort House. Japanese and Korean prostitutes were housed there for the comfort of the army and navy. Officers privileges were at night while enlisted men found their comfort during the day. One particular night we heard a great disturbance coming from that direction followed by several pistol shots. The ruckus settled down after a while and things became normal until about three in the morning when we were awakened by the guards bringing a Jap soldier into our cell. Even in the dark of the night we could tell that the guy was a battered pulp but it was not until daylight that we could really see his hideous condition. He was propped up and immobile in a sitting position. When someone tried to find a pulse, we realized he was dead and with this slight touch he topped over on the floor. It was then about time for the morning meal and our rice would soon be showing up. We shoved the soldier back into a sitting position in the darkest corner of the cell and opened his eye lids and pulled his cheeks slightly back into a smile, just as the rice boy showed up. The familiar balls were passed in as usual except that we explained to the rice boy that the newly arrived soldier was in bad shape and that we thought he should be given several balls and perhaps a cup of soup. We got away with it for three more meals before a guard investigated closely and pronounced him unqualified for further meals. He too was hauled away by natives. His crime was having tried to crash the lineup to the Comfort House across the street during the time that only officers were permitted.

The dead soldier's chief assailant, we learned later, was the "Ulta Methul" of despicability, the prince of darkness, named Wada. Of all the fanatical sons of bitches among the Kempe Tai garrison, he was the worst. He had the ability to twist any action, any remark or gesture made by a prisoner into something of a personal affront and had no reluctance to inflict imaginative punishment like making the offender sit for hours on his upright heels, kicks and slaps in vital areas or making him drink gallons of water until the prisoner vomited. He would require the whole cell block to sit at attention in utter silence for his full eight hour stint of duty. Some of the other guards even vaguely disapproved of him. He was a complete degenerate.

One day while a prisoner from Kannapolis, NC, Ronnie Mull, was outside the cell serving our rice and Wada was in charge, he began picking on Ronnie. He kicked him a couple of times and in what Ronnie perceived to be a playful mood, slapped at him in the style of an American boxer. Ronnie was a recent captive and in fairly good health and not recognizing the significant of this, he began to pantomime, to some extent, the stance of a boxer himself. This shadow boxing led to a heated fist fight completely out of control with partisan groups watching both sides. Wada was incensed that Ronnie would fight back and more so because he was getting the worst of it.

From inside the cell we were reluctant to applaud but nevertheless bursting with pride and admiration. Suffering from humiliation and realizing he did not have complete approval from his own men, Wada reached for a large club with which to attack his upstart opponent. One of the guards at that moment fired his pistol and brought the combat to a halt. Ronnie was ushered back into the cell by protective guards but no further rice was served that day. Everyone of us would gladly have given up several meals for the gratification of seeing Wada so thoroughly smashed. Ronnie was to pay for his actions later on, but we couldn't have been prouder of Sgt. Mull.

In contrast to Wada, one of the friendliest guards we had at this time was a little fat faced Japanese named Kujushima who had a sense of humor which most did not have. Kuji probably today could be an entertaining chef at an American chain of Japanese restaurants. He was misplaced in the Kempe Tai. He had a fascination for Hollywood and continually asked questions about it. He could walk like Charlie Chaplin but never performed when other guards were present. Such actions led him into a state of confidentiality with us which we enjoyed and pursued vigorously. We began to take liberties with him that would have been disastrous with any of the other guards. This reliance on each other's discretion prompted us to suggest jokingly that he lead us in an escape attempt through Japanese lines. In return we would sponsor him in Hollywood. My father was a Packard automobile dealer and

I generously offered to give him one when we reached Safety. He was familiar with Packardo. His Emperor had several Packardos. His eyes would brighten with delusions of grandeur until the fantasy passed. He was convinced that upon arrival in America he would be beheaded and our intended bribes came to nothing as we of course knew they would.

Another of our interesting guards was an older man named Tsukahara, a former teacher of English in a Japanese Middle School. He was about forty years old. His English was very formal and cautiously spoken. His sentences like "Soldiers of other side, how is your good health today?" broke us up. "Japan shall be winning the contest nervously. Many Christmases soon shall come until you are returned domicile."

He like Kuji was miscast as a fierce Kempe Tai. He was an unmarried romantic, an admirer of Shakespeare whom he frequently quoted. In many ways he was an honest old maid.

Once, during an intense allied air raid with Tsuki standing guard, he, as was the custom, ran to his bomb shelter while we weathered the storm in our wooden shack. At this particular time there were several native prisoners in with us among whom was one named Gando. Gando was in excellent health, had a fine physique and above average native intelligence. When Tsukihara disappeared into the shelter, Gando jumped up and kicked the door, breaking the lock which wasn't hard to do, ran outside and implored us to escape with him. The nearest allied troops were no less than two hundred and fifty miles away. In our weaked condition we stood no chance at all of slipping through the Jap infested jungles to safety. Gando was adamant and screamed at us to accompany him. In disgust he took off alone. We learned later that after months of travail and distress in the jungle, he made it.

After the war, Murphy wrote me that Gando had given allied intelligence an enormous amount of accurate and vital information about Jap installations and personnel. He was awarded the Australian Loyalty Medal and a cash reward for his services.

The sad thing after the escape was that old Tsukihara, the

dignified English teacher, was dealt with most severely by the Japanese authorities. The indignities they cast on him were almost inhuman; punishment for a situation that he could hardly have controlled, but he stayed on as a guard and we were inclined to sympathize with him because the same thing could have happened to any of the guards, yet he became an outcast. We only wished that Wada had been on duty.

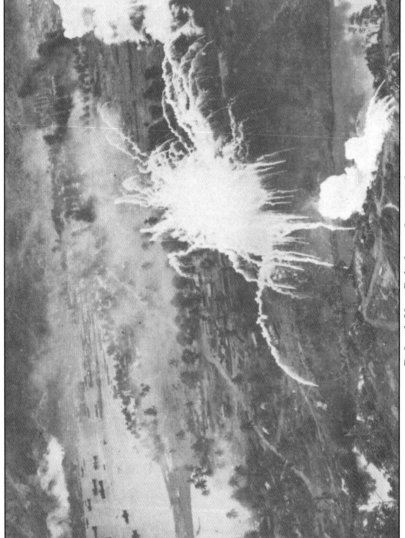

Rabaul, New Britain under attack.

# Chapter 14

Allied bombing had been rather brisk all during November and into December. As Christmas approached we advised the guards that Christian principals would probably be observed by the Allies on the 25th and that no bombing should be expected. On Christmas morning the unused extra Benjo bucket was allowed to be placed outside the cell bearing a sign that Murphy had printed in Japanese characters literally translated as "Christmas Gift." By mid-morning the sign had attracted the attention of several magnanimous visitors and a welcomed collection of half eaten papaya and potato skins had been received.

"Christmas isn't going to be so bad after all," said Charlie Lanphier. "I'm staking a claim on that big piece of yellow papaya I see out there."

I was a potato peeling freak and announced my intention to take my share in peelings.

The words were just out of my mouth when the air raid sirens went off all over the area. Another damn raid and on Christmas morning! Our guard Matsuoka took one hateful look at us and said, "Americano hetai yasumi ni!" American soldiers never rest. With that he took our Christmas Gift Bucket and ran for the air raid shelter. The bastard!

If allied raids on Rabaul had been brisk during November and December, they were too numerous to count in January and February 1944. Attacks by low level short range aircraft sent a distinct message that our forces were moving north. We caught sight of allied fighter planes and A-20's that had to be flying out of advanced airfields. Aircraft carriers were sending many dive bombers to attack Simson Harbor. Otaka sneaked by the cell one day and reported that Blanche Bay was a mess with sunken Japanese ships. He also came by one night and stealthily threw a dozen or more fat potato peelings in through the bars. That was every bit as welcome as the news he brought. A few days later a flight of A-20's and P-38's dropped thousands of para-frag bombs all over the area. We were able to see a few of the little parachutes floating down from the low level onto the Emperor's stronghold.

I winked at Tom Doyle and said, "By God, they'll be coming in here to get us one of these days soon, and I'm gonna be embarrassed for U.S. Marines to see this place looking so shitty. How about a couple of your sons-a-bitches cleaning up the room before some big ape out of Paris Island comes in here and puts us on K.P. duty."

"What makes you crazy asses think the Nips would just run off and leave us sittin' here during an invasion? First thing those silly bastards will do is take those Samurai swords and cut your fucking head off Farnell," said Joe Nason.

"Go back to sleep, Nason; you're gonna die before they get here anyway," said Murphy.

This banter went on for some time until a serious Ishamura, one of the better guards, came over and made a pronouncement.

"Our Colonel say big raid come tomorrow. We have chance to shoot many American planes. Catch many prisoners. Maybe you see some your friends tomorrow."

He wasn't joking. On the first of March all hell broke loose. Somehow the Nips had received word that the 5th Air Force, the 13th Air Force, the Navy and the Marines were going to clobber the town of Rabaul and everything around it. The fireworks stared at breakfast time. One humongous flight of heavies rained 1,000 pounders all over the place. Our three cells rocked and rolled for over an hour. Then we heard shells coming in from out at sea. One series of shells walked up to within a hundred yards of the prison with the final salvo exploding a hundred yards beyond us. Every Nip gun in the area was returning the fire. We stayed paralyzed until five Kempe Tai soldiers rushed over to us, unlocked the doors, handcuffed us and marched us out to where we had built the huge bomb shelter near the street in front. It didn't take any prodding to get us down in that hole. About 30 Jap soldiers were already down there just as concerned as we were. Deafening explosion after explosion with increasing intensity rocked the town. It was impossible to hear anyone speak except in a shout, although no one had much to say anyway, except Professor Sugden who screamed about the roar, "Serious matter, ain't it?"

No one thought that was funny. Smoke filled our shelter. We heard fire raging from above. A large cistern of water must have been hit as streams of it came flowing down into our pit. Drowning became a possibility if we got trapped. Whining aircraft motors, and swooshing of falling bombs and the terrifying whistling of naval shells all homogenized into unearthly sounds. Hour after hour of this with no let up until about noon when a slight lull brought a dozen screaming Japs into the shelter ordering the prisoners to come up to the surface. Some who could hardly walk were hurried by the butts of Jap rifles. What we saw at the top was indescribable. Nothing was standing upright including twenty four inch diameter coconut trees. A fire storm swept the town, and God knows what the Jap airfields and bivouac areas and the harbor looked like.

Two flat bed trucks with motors racing and drivers screaming stood by as guards literally threw us, handcuffed, up into the beds. No on seemed to know what was going on including the guards. Someone must have because the trucks raced wide open down dirt roads rolling and twisting around bomb craters and fires, all but throwing us off the back of the truck. A few planes were still in the area and more were returning. As we reached the comparative safety of some heavy woods the intensity of bombing and strafing began to pick up again. We were traveling to higher ground on a washed out one lane road with a good overhang of trees and thank God for it. Just before being loaded on the truck we had been blindfolded sloppily and were able to get a partial view of what was going on.

Up the hill we went for twenty or thirty minutes afraid to make any comment for fear of the strange guards riding with us and fuming like locomotives. A level grade in the road brought the trucks to a halt, and we hurriedly unloaded.

"Into the cave, into the cave!" the guards shouted as they prodded us with their rifles.

The cave was approximately forty feet long and only about four feet wide. It was unlighted and damp. There were a few logs on the floor that were hard to see and made for difficult footing. There were no supports along the sides or top of the cave. We crushed ourselves into it body to body with no room other than to stand. To conserve handcuffs just before entering the Japs cuffed two prisoners together, making walking more difficult. When we filled the cave completely a large blanket was fastened to the entrance permitting no view to the outside nor light to come inside. So we stood and stood and stood, unable to sit down in the cramped quarters while the raid continued for two more days without let up. We were well out of any target zone and fairly safe from bombs, but in a terrible sanitary mess and had been given no water for over 48 hours. We managed to cool our parched throats by gradually inching out one at a time to the front of the cave and chewing on the rain drenched blanket covering the entrance. If someone managed to squeeze into a sitting position, his handcuffed partner had to lean in an accommodating position to take the pressure off his wrists. Joe Holguin found a piece of wire on the floor of the cave and bent it into the semblance of a key that would unlock the cuffs. This was quite a relief. From time to time the guards would call us all out for a roll call; a thoroughly unnecessary process, but the fresh air was a relief. When a roll call and inspection was announced, we quickly snapped our handcuffs back in place. Joe Nason was about 6 feet 3 inches tall and his partner was a tubercular Chinese who stood no more than 5 feet 2 inches. During one unanticipated inspection everyone snapped their handcuffs back in place as quickly as possible before coming outside. Nason and the Chinaman were standing close to the front and had little time to react so that when we all lined up, Nason's right wrist was coupled to the Chinaman's right wrist leaving them facing opposite directions. Joe's explanation to the infuriated guard as to how he twisted his legs over the Chinaman's head and back around under his left elbow to arrive at this condition was about the only thing we had to laugh at for a long time, and we all busted our sides. We quit laughing when Joe and the Chinaman got a thorough bashing; however, we never let Joe live it down.

On the morning of March 4, 1944, after three full days and nights of standing up in the cave without food or water, the attacks on Rabaul leveled off and we were again called outside and this time we were allowed to sit down while a conference was going on among two or three Jap officers. The roll was called after a while, and we were separated into two groups. The first group consisted of Doyle, Farnell, Sugden, Evans, Stookey, Chelli, Barron, Harris, Kicera, Kershner, Hill Borders, Mayberry, Berry, Barthoff, Brendoz, Mull, McLeaf, Kuhn, Kobig and Fenwick. This list is incomplete but represents the bulk of the group.

The remaining thirty of us were returned to the cave while the first group was again placed on a truck and carried away. We only had a few minutes to say good-bye to some of the best friends I'd ever had, particularly the three members of my crew: Doyle, Sugden and Farnell. The rest of my crew had been shipped to Japan. We asked the guards where the departing group was going but got no intelligent answer other than, "To a safer place."

We continued to ask about them for several months. Our question seemed to irritate the guards and we were told to shut up and forget about that group. They wanted no more reference to it. We strongly suspected that they had been executed judging from the attitude of the guards. The incident was a very hot potato and they wanted nothing to do with it. We never learned a damned thing until the war was over and even then it was a vague and unsatisfactory account.

One more day and night in this Tunnel Hill Road cave and the rest of us were moved to a more satisfactory site on the side of a shallow ravine that we soon named Death Valley because of the growing number of guys succumbing to death by starvation, disease and neglect. Most of the deceased would lapse into a coma and linger for as long as a week when at the end they would unconsciously bite the air as if struggling for a last breath. They went peacefully and I believe painlessly, but it was heartbreaking to watch so many fine young boys die under such foul conditions. Literally and figuratively we could only take it lying down, make the most of it and pray we would not be the next to go.

I felt I had not prayed hard enough during the summer of 1944. My edema had me swollen up like a balloon. My vision was blurred and my energy was nil. I suffered short blackout periods never really knowing for how long. Joe Holguin was a charmer and got on with the guards better than most. During one of my blackouts, I was told that Joe cajoled a Jap corpsman to look at me which he did and they say he gave me an injection of some sort, quite possibly a placebo. I hung on for a few days in semi-consciousness but began picking young green leaves off an overhanging tree and eating them. My edema left me after a week and I returned to my former skin and bones.

Our Death Valley compound was one large room hastily constructed with a rough floor and tin roof supported by two by fours narrowly spaced on three sides. The rear again was a dirt bank with a small cave dug into it for air raid protection.

Joe Holguin's broken back had mended somewhat leaving him in a stooped position, but without pain. The hole in his lower jaw just in front of his adams apple penetrating through to his tongue was still festering. The drainage was awful looking and obstructed his speech somewhat. Joe and I sat next to each other day after day and were warm friends.

One morning a strafing P-38 flew up our ravine surprising everyone. There had been no alarm. As I jumped up from my seat on the floor my bony knee caught Joe square in the jaw. He was scrambling for the cave at the same time when the blow hit him. The corruption that came out of his jaw puddled on the floor and looked terrible, but we noticed it contained a small piece of bone. Joe smiled, looked at me and said, "Doctor Mac, I believe you've performed a successful operation. My damned jaw feels fine." The wound healed over in a matter of a few days and I felt I had unintentionally repaid him for his gift of my placebo.

During that summer we lost our friends at a rate of about one a week for several months and the number of survivors was down to around twenty.

# Chapter 15

Most of the same guards were assigned to us day after day, and we began to know them much better. Discipline became somewhat relaxed except that for some reason they began waking us up in the middle of the night for a roll call which was entirely unnecessary. Nevertheless during the day we would chat with them in a relaxed manner. They each knew about Babe Ruth, they knew about Lindbergh, Henry Ford and George Washington. Someone mentioned Barnum and Bailey's circus. They were fascinated with circuses, so we decided to put one on for them. Murphy pretended to hypnotize me after which I would become rigid while standing and then fall stiffly backward being caught just before hitting the floor. Someone did a slight of hand trick, Todd tried to hang by his heels from a rafter and fell, I did a soft shoe tap and they called me Fred Astaire. Joe Nason recited, "Casey at the Bat," none of which the guards understood but enjoyed immensely. Charlie Lanphier and I harmonized an old church hymn, "In the Garden." Four cigarettes were passed in by Ishamura, who was completely entranced. Other guards heard about our act and demanded a rerun. The Death Valley circus played for about a week. The income was close to a full package of Homeri cigarettes and some of the guard's left over cucumber pickles. The diversion was more profitable than the cigarettes or pickles, and our finale, "Mississippi Mid," sung by the whole prison group and accompanied by foot stomping and backslapping was a great morale builder.

There was a cook house about three hundred yards down the edge of the ravine. We could hear chopping and slicing and pots and pans banging together at quiet times. The intrepid coast watcher Murphy was sorely tempted. It was easy to get out of the cell if one wanted to. One of the corrugated tin barriers at the entrance to the shelter was loose and could easily be raised enough for a man to slip out under it. Execution was the firmly promised penalty for an escape attempt. Escape from New Britain would have been utterly impossible even if one were in good health. Murph didn't want to escape. Murph wanted the cook house. He didn't tell the whole group he was going to try it for fear of complicity if he were caught; but he did tell three of us.

The guard box was at a blind angle from the side of the cave entrance with the loose panel. It was hard for a guard sitting in his box outside to see the full length and breadth of the overall cell itself and impossible to see the cave entrance in the rear of the cell. Guard duty was just as boring to them as sitting out the war was to us. The fact that the war was going north was gradually dawning on them although they wouldn't admit it. Some began to take cat naps while on duty at night. Others kept up the facade that they would soon be called to active duty in the invasion of Australia. That is not to say that the cat nappers were becoming more tolerant, as a matter of fact those guys were basically more dangerous because of the frustration based on suicidal dedication to their Emperor and a combination of their Buddhist and Shintoist inheritance. Regardless of the two attitudes Murphy still was willing to chance it and on one of those dark nights when everything was status quo, Murph quietly broke out alone and found his way perilously in the dark to the empty cook house. He gouged himself with left over rice, a raw vegetable or two and finally found some canned goods. Having no way to open them, he slug them in his Fundoshi (loin cloth) and sneaked back up the hill, reentering the passage to the cave and assumed his normal sitting place in the corner. I was amazed that he had gotten away with it, but very thankful not just for his sake either; because I'm sure we all would have suffered if he had been caught. Murph was very generous with his stolen can goods, which amounted to two cans of milk and a little canned fruit. Those of us who were not asleep got a couple of swigs of milk and a taste of fruit. We got them opened with a loose nail from the floor boards.

Murph tried it again the next night and again got away with it, but now we had a big problem what to do with a collection of about six empty cans.

The only possible solution was to put them in the Benjo bucket. This meant that one of us would have to carry the bucket to the garden under the close watch of one of the guards and risk him seeing tin cans splashing out of our bucket in the large catch basin. There could be no satisfactory explanation we knew, and no one wanted to be the "Benjo Boy" that day. Finally the slickest of slick, Alphonso Quinones, Tucson, Arizona's own, volunteered. Al was the good natured pilot of a P-38 shot down on his first mission by a lucky shot. Al was flying on the right side of a formation of 38's being attacked from way out on the left side by a lone Zero. It was pure bad luck and an undeserved victory for the Zero.

Al was a good story teller, a good actor who could put you in hysterics when he would get emotional about his bad luck, speaking a mile a minute in English and shifting back and forth into Spanish. His parents had come to Arizona from their native Puerto Rico. On several occasions just to liven things up Al jumped up into the middle of the room screaming at the top of his voice and pretending to have gone insane. The guards never knew what to make of him and sometimes I didn't either; but we all admired him.

It was time for the dynamite loaded honeybucket to be carried out. Al got a thumbs up from us all as he heaved the bucket off the floor and stood perfectly still; giving each of us around the room a confidential wink while the guard waited impatiently outside. Off he went on his second most dangerous mission. It took about fifteen minutes to get to the garden, empty the bucket and return to the cell. No one spoke, fearing the worst. A guard named Yamasta accompanied him and Yamasata was Mr. Vicious. How was Al going to handle it? The guards never let you get more than a few feet from them. Although the bucket was heavy Al made an extra struggling effort all the way up the path just as though he was about to fall and drop it. When he saw the catch basin ahead and about twenty yards away he put on a fantastic stumbling act, picking up speed, leaving the guard well behind him and crashed down on his knees just as he emptied the bucket, milk cans and all, with the guard still trying to catch up without losing his dignity. Al rose to his feet and resignedly stood over the cistern waiting for the verdict from floating or non-floating tin cans. They non-floated and Al walked blithely back down the path jabbering who knows what in Spanish.

Native prisoners were often placed in the cell with us and received equal status. Now the number of natives was growing due in some part, I believe, to the fact that the Allies were clearly on the offensive and intuition was causing their loyalty to vacillate. They no doubt had heard through the grapevine about the allied landing at Cape Gloucester at the other end of New Britain three hundred miles south, although we were unaware of it at this time. As more natives were imprisoned the Kempe Tai decided to build a small annex to our cell and house all native prisoners there. There were still some among us who could walk and were strong enough to serve as rice boys. This meant not only serving us but the natives as well. In addition to our ball of rice we were now also getting a small can of thin soup served in used tin cans holding about four ounces of the liquid. It came from the cook house in a wooden bucket like the rice. At rare times the soup contained not just potato leaves but some left over chopped vegetables most of which sank to the bottom of the bucket. The rice boy had the option of scooping the watery soup off the top or ladling some of the vegetables to go with it. Sgt. Escoe Palmer of Gainesville, Ga., a recent captive, was in fairly good health and served the food for many weeks. Palmer, being from the south and not realizing what a good potential ally the natives were destined to be, never served them from the bottom of the bucket nor did he go too heavy on the size of their rice balls. Since they were short timers as opposed to us, Palmer felt justified in his discrimination and we had it good until they complained bitterly and an Oriental half caste was appointed rice boy by the guards, and Palmer's hey day was over. This small amount of additional nourishment was a slight boost to our health and spirit except in the case of Joe Nason of Westbury, Mass., the gaunt six foot three pilot of a Navy S.B.D.--Nason was a Dartmouth graduate, who refused to learn much of the Japanese language and relied solely on others to converse with the Japs or the natives. His depression worried us and we bet he wasn't going to make it, but Joe hung on independently day after day.

Esco Palmer had seen every cowboy movie that was produced between 1930 and 1940. He remembered them in detail and didn't hesitate to tell us about them at all hours of the day and night. Some were fairly interesting, but his constant droning on and on in his nasal voice more often put us to sleep than entertain us. Most every other conversation was about food. We all solemnly swore that after the war, if we survived, we would go to a cooks and bakers school and become chefs. We were dead serious about it. We also thought about the millions of cigarette butts thrown away in hotel lobbies and offices that could be collected and reprocessed. We could undersell the hell out of R. J. Reynolds and make a fortune on the side while cooking and baking and eating and eating and eating.

I remembered the poem by Kipling, "The Road to Mandalay," which was set to music. I sang it poorly, but sang it. Murphy remembered an Australian poem by Banjo Patterson called "The Man from Snowy River," and recited it with wild gesturing. The colt of a thoroughbred, "Old Regret," had gotten out of the stockade and joined, as Murphy said "The wild bush bastards." The poem revolved around the Australian stockmen's effort to recapture the prized colt. It was very exciting and relived the boredom.

We had a stubby pencil and a collection of empty Jap cigarette packages. The back of the empty packs could be used as writing paper. Recipes were concocted and written down as a fantasy. I have the collection to this day, an excellent sample of which is:

Take one suckling pig (larger is desired) Soak for 2 weeks in a mixture of salt, vinegar, bruised garlic and juniper berries (or gin)
*Stuff with Yorkshire pudding and pint of oysters*
*Surround with cored apples*
*Serve with mashed potatoes and pork gravy*
*Cream topped fruit cake for dessert.*
A healthy rasher of that ought to put some meat on starving bones.

That gruesome recipe was one of the more conventual ones. There were many more that combined ingredients that would turn the stomach of the hardest ditch digger today. In our unprofessional way I guess the only things that mattered in a recipe was that it contain digestible food regardless of aesthetic value. And as for aesthetics, the thought that frustrated us the most was remembering all the food that was thrown away in army mess halls. Even in our own homes; peelings, bones, scraps, leftovers scraped into garbage pails. What a banquet these leftovers would make for us now. One day's garbage from an ordinary household would feed us for weeks.

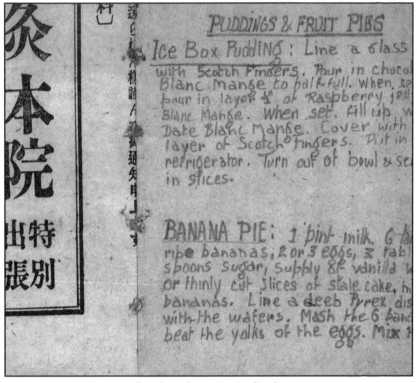

PUDDINGS & FRUIT PIES

Ice Box Pudding : Line a glass
with Scotch Fingers. Pour in chocol
Blanc Mange to half-full. When, se
pour in layer ¼" of Raspberry jell
Blanc Mange. When set, fill up w
Date Blanc Mange. Cover with
layer of Scotch Fingers. Put in
refrigerator. Turn out of bowl & se
in slices.

BANANA PIE: 1 pint milk. 6 to
ripe bananas, 2 or 3 eggs, 3 tab
spoons sugar, supply of vanilla w
or thinly cut slices of stale cake, h
bananas. Line a deep pyrex dis
with the wafers. Mash the 6 ban
beat the yolks of the eggs. Mix t

**Our imaginary menu book.**

# Chapter 16

A slight turn for the better seemed to arrive with the appointment of a new Kempe Tai commander. We somehow got word to him that we should be allowed to come outside and plant a garden; grow vegetables and in short, make ourselves useful. We sold the idea, and for a brief period those of us who were able to walk were given this privilege. We were given some bean and melon seeds and permitted to struggle up a steep hill to a plateau to do the plowing and planting. We worked with our bare hands and a few pointed sticks. Having no clothing except our fundoshi our bodies soaked up the glorious sunshine. A few scoops of fertilizer from the Benjo drums assured us of a mighty harvest some day. After a few weeks however, the Kempe Tai commander was again replaced and our days in the sun were over sans harvest. Offsetting the failure to make a vegetable crop was the fact that we got a little sunshine, stole a few of the Japs vegetables and on one occasion I found two sea gull eggs and unhesitantly swallowed them raw. Sometimes a grain of humor was worth ten grains of rice.

Following that rather pleasant interlude one day a soldier appeared at our cell with a few leaves of tobacco he had stolen from a native garden. He asked a marvelous question, "Do you know how to make cigarettes?"

Murphy and I were the first to say we not only knew how, but would be glad to demonstrate our talent. I put great emphasis on the fact that I came from the south where Camels, Luckies, Chesterfields and Old Golds were made. He knew those names and admitted having smoked them when they were available before the war. A deal was struck, and he handed over the leaves.

He supplied us with two small nails and two small joints of bamboo, a three-inch piece of cloth and two small blocks of wood. We inserted the nails through the bamboo, glued the cloth loosely around the two joints, leaving a slight hammock life depression between the two, then nailed this to the two blocks of wood for support. We spent an hours chopping the leaves into shreds, put them down in the three-inch hammock and rolled the two joints which shaped the tobacco properly. We then cut Japanese newspaper to size, glued one edge, inserted it in the roller and encapsulated the shredded tobacco. After snipping off the excess at the ends, we had a pretty professional looking cigarette--about forty of them.

That afternoon when the soldier returned he was very proud of our work and his idea. Typically, he rewarded us with one cigarette to be cut in half and enjoyed by me and Murph. It was better than the few butts we had heretofore scrounged off the ground when sweeping up the area. It was a hell of a lot better than the straw mat we had been shredding and smoking from time to time. The mat, incidentally, got smaller and smaller over the weeks that we had it and its gradual demise mystified our keepers.

Now Murph and I had a half of a virgin cigarette given to us by this generous Nip. We smiled, thanked him and said, "Y'awl come back, ya hear." In a few days he did come back and this time he was loaded with leaves. He cleaned out some poor native's garden with no twinge of conscience; I'm sure ours didn't twinge a great deal either, because it looked like we were now in business.

"How many cigarettes can you make from these leaves, horio (prisoner)?" he asked.

We slowly counted the leaves, went into deep concentration, gazed off into space and came up with an answer. We told him we could produce exactly one hundred and ninety-six little beauties. The contract actually netted nearer two hundred and thirty, which gave me and Murph a hidden profit of thirty-four plus the one with which he again generously rewarded us. The wheels of the marketing department of McMurria, Murphy Manufacturing Co., (M.M.M.C.) came into action while our customer gather up his loot.

"Heitai San, you like real number one cigarette all same honorable Yamamota smoke?"

"Whanin sumting," he replied. "What do you mean?"

We told him if he would give us the proper supplies we could make a cigarette as good as or better than the Admiral of the Japanese Navy smoked. We would give it the old North Carolina treatment. All we would need was as decent pair of scissors, some cardboard, a bowl of sugar and two bowls of rice. We made a big thing out of sugar curing leaves, i.e. soaking them in a gallon water with two teaspoons of sugar for the leaves and a cup full· for M.M.M.C. private consumption. One grain of cooked rice would glue two cigarettes and a half a bowl would glue two or three hundred; caveat emptor behind bars. With the card board we cut out and glued together a stiff box that held twenty cigarettes. Murph had some artistic talent and was able to cut out the hiragana syllabaries representing the soldiers name and to glue them to the box. We also cut out his rank insignia and placed it below his name. From the soldier's reaction, when we presented him with nine and a half flip top boxes of twenty stogies each, you would have thought we had discovered gold. We had.

In no time at all various soldiers would come by with stolen leaves and ask us to make them cigarettes and personalized boxes. Some of the names were difficult to reproduce in hiragana. Insignias were no problem at all. The written language is such that one character can have many meanings depending on the character preceding or following it. A near disaster happened when the spelling of one soldier's name literally translated appeared more like "Crazy Goose" than Ozawa. The innocent mistake was soon forgiven, but the epithet stuck to the humiliated solider for several weeks. The surplus sugar and rice was no less enjoyable. Overall those status symbols allowed our customers to overlook the fact that we were stealing them blind. Our guards had to approve of our activity because we were working for their buddies; therefore, smoking in the cell became acceptable. We shared our loot with the other prisoners. The nicotine took a little of the edge off of our hunger pangs, but there was an even greater benefit to come.

It was custom of the cook house to frequently send between meal snacks to the guards standing duty. This was most chopped eggplant, sweet potatoes, cucumber pickles or brine soaked cherries. They weren't always hungry but seemed always short of cigarettes. We weren't audacious enough to out and out bargain with them, but in many cases when we politely offered them a smoke, naturally at snack time, they in turn would share their snack; not out of generosity, but because they simply didn't want it, lucky symbiosis. We could sense their boredom and growing dislike for the same old food day in and day out. We had experienced the same thing before we were shot down and were constantly fed canned corn beef and powdered milk and eggs back in Port Moresby, Oh, for some of that now!

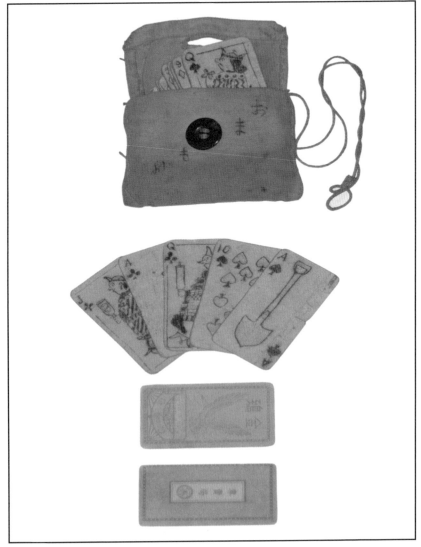

**Playing cards made from Japanese cigarette packs.**

# Chapter 17

In late 1944 and early 1945, the Allies considered the campaign against Rabaul as stabilized and were taking the war north. We were aware of it because the conversations we overhead frequently included a reference to "Philippine," which we knew had to mean the Philippine Islands. We also heard frequent reference to "B ne ju ku," which meant B-29 the Boeing Superfort. Rabaul was stabilized but by no means free from attack from the sea or the air. Harassment continued though not with its former intensity. The Japanese never ceased to insist that they were still on the offensive, but an ever so slight change in their attitude became obvious. The same guards went on and off duty routinely. There was no shifting of personnel. We came to know intimate details of their lives and they of ours. Perhaps a Japanese victory by now seemed a little less likely to them, although there was no doubt in our minds that the enemy would fight to the last man and regardless of the time it took for a clear cut decision. Ten more years did not seem unrealistic. Day to day survival was still the name of our game, and food was the key to survival. No prisoner weighed more than a hundred pounds and someone died every month.

Looking out of our cell, not more than a hundred yards away was a veritable mountain of coconuts, whichthe Japs used to extract oil and make soap. They were nevertheless edible and naturally the object of much prisoner lust.

On three different occasions when Okano, "the Irishman," was on duty at night, we cajoled him into passing a nut into the cell. The Irishman was a rather stupid guy and on the whole unpredictable. His moods changed rapidly, but it was our good fortune to catch him on a high three nights in a row. He even passed a screwdriver in with the nut allowing us to open it and consume it quickly before anyone caught him in what would have been considered a treasonable act. The hard white meat was delicious and smelled even more so, and we hoped his generosity would continue. After the third night Okano felt that it was too dangerous, and he called it off. His mood changed thereafter, and he often threatened to confess the whole matter to his superiors; whereby, he and the prisoners would, without doubt, be severely punished.

Shortly thereafter the Allies entered into a project of destroying the hundreds of acres of vegetable gardens around Rabaul. U.S. and Australian bombers came over and dropped used motor oil on them then set them on fire with napalm. The same army that killed thousands of Americans with a sneak attack on Pearl Harbor considered the burning of their gardens as completely inhumane. Their retribution could only fall on the POW's. As a consequence, orders came down prohibiting any further rice to be served to us. Instead each two prisoners was given a coconut to be divided every morning, noon and night. Our lust for the oily meat subsided at the end of the first day. After a couple of years of the soft digestible rice, our stomachs were unprepared for the harsh roughage. Dysentery set in with a vengeance and increased the death rate noticeably. We ate nothing but coconut for six weeks until the order was rescinded, and we went back on rice. The only pleasant recollection of that era  was the delicious aroma of the coconut when thrown into the hot coals of the smoke pot used to ward off mosquitoes.

Bombing Mission – Rabaul
This time we are on the target.

# Chapter 18

Cassava trees are grown extensively in the South Pacific Islands. The roots of the trees grow near the surface of the ground and when they reach the approximate size of a large candle and are about 18 to 20 inches long, they can be cooked and eaten, and although they are not very tasty, they do have some food value. It is the basis of a manufactured product called Tapioca. They taste a little like a very bland Irish potato and are very starchy. The Japanese harvested a great deal of these cassava roots and mixed them with their rice in order to stretch their food supply. The Japanese soldiers generally objected to this as they are very fond of and hold pure white rice in a special reverence. This special attachment to pure white rice was exhibited by the action of some of the cooks who illegally failed to mix 10% barley (moogi) in with their rice which they were instructed to do. Barley provides certain vitamins which are not contained in rice and the authorities issued orders that barley or moogi should be mixed with rice for added nourishment. Because of the unpopularity of this order, certain cooks would, on occasion, withhold the barley and dispose of it by feeding it to the prisoners. In spite of the scant ration we received, we nevertheless felt it was a great boon to us to be fed the barley, and we encouraged this breach of orders, believing that it was more nutritious than white rice.

But back to the cassava roots; the Japs didn't like it mixed with their rice either, so on occasions when the supply of cassava was built up, the prisoners were given pure cassava without rice. Now in our effort to improve the cassava diet we suggested to the guards that we could make bread out of it. They were surprised and very enthusiastic over this possibility and promptly offered to let us try it. Our constant concern and fondest hope was to be associated with food in any manner possible thereby presenting an opportunity for theft.

After being directed to have a go at baking bread, our first move was to requisition an amount of cassava far in excess of what was honestly required. Experience in the cigarette trade had taught us that we would be rewarded for our efforts at the barest minimum; therefore, the excess cassava could wind up as advance commission to the ingenious bakers.

Now with several dozen roots in hand we next asked for a couple of pieces of screen wire which we attached over a small wooden frame. We then cut the long roots into thin slices resembling a poker chip and placed them in the hot sun for three days to dry out. On the fourth day we laboriously grated the dry chips over the screen wire and thus produced flour. We then asked for an excessive supply of salt, sugar and several medium ripe and one rotten coconut; having no idea that milk might be available. Fresh milk of course wasn't, but the guards came up with two cans of evaporated milk; which we diluted with the medium ripe coconut milk. Green coconut milk is effervescent and ripe coconut milk is soapy and undesirable.

The milk from the over ripe or rotten coconut was placed in a small container to which a little sugar was added and allowed to ferment. We used the mold thus produced as a form of yeast to make the milk and flour mixture rise. In the meantime, we had dug a small pit outside our cell, lined it with rock and built a fire in the pit. We molded the dough into small tin cans that had been greased with copra oil, extinguished the fire, placed the dough in the pit and covered the top with a piece of corrugated roofing metal. The hot rocks in the enclosed pit provided an excellent oven and in a mater of 30 or 40 minutes the smell of the baking bread became obvious over a wide area and Japanese soldiers began to appear from everywhere. As expected the "six loaves and no fishes" were immediately devoured by the delighted Japanese and nary a bit for the poor baker. Little did they know that their share of the supplies was about equal to what we had stealthily consumed in another form. i.e., we cooked the raw stolen roots in the smoke pot after dark.

A similar situation arose when the prisoners killed a large snake under our cell and requested that we be allowed to eat it. The guards vehemently ridiculed the suggestion but after seeing the skinned and dressed meat, offered to cook it for us and wound up. eating it themselves; giving us a very weak soup made from the meat of the snake, alibiing that the meat had cooked away and the soup was all that was left.

I have previously mentioned a Korean civilian prisoner named Otaka who joined my crew as a prisoner in Wewak and who followed us subsequently to the Island of Kariru at the tragic Catholic mission station and from there to Rabaul. Otaka seemed to share our fortune and fate for the first six months, because he had vainly tried to escape and was initially severely dealt with; but as time went on and he realized the futility of returning from the S.W. Pacific to Korea, some 1,500 miles through enemy territory, he became complacent and resigned himself to captivity and tended to make the best of things in his uneducated way. His native intellect and instinct for survival prompted him to cooperate with the Japs and settle for the status quo. His many menial tasks included things that put him in daily contact with the prisoners in his status as a trusty. This status allowed him sufficient latitude to grasp what was going on in the battle of Rabaul far greater than anything the prisoners could imagine. We could hear the bombs falling and the shellings from Allied PT boats and submarines, but we had small conception of the effect of these forays--Otaka, on the other hand, could at times see the results--the wrecks in the harbor, the devastated airfields with their crippled armada and the bombed out installation. When circumstances dictated that he be in our vicinity he made an effort to encourage us with the news that the Japs were taking a beating around Rabaul. It was impossible for us to keep quiet about Allied successes reported by Otaka, and we took great pleasure in accurately predicting to our captors the results of the Allied raids although we never revealed our source of information. We so successfully pinpointed such results that the Japs believe we must have radio communications with our forces. When accused of this we encouraged their suspicion to the point that one day they entered our cell and small bombshelter with a pick and shovel and attempted to dig up our radio equipment. A reverse frustration for their side. Chalk up one for the prisoners.

Rabaul under low level attack. Note ships in harbor.

# Chapter 19

Communication between people with different languages can provide amusing misinterpretations. We found ourselves talking Australian, New Zealand and Pidgin English. Most of the Japs had some knowledge of English as it is a required subject in some of their middle schools. They were anxious to perfect it and constantly practiced it on us, while we hoped to learn as much Japanese as possible as a security measure and for convenience. We both needed to know Pidgin English to converse with the natives.

I once heard a Japanese officer talking over a telephone at the top of his voice as though speaking to someone a long distance away. He kept saying "Moshi Moshiee" which sounded for all the world like he was saying "Porse Morsbee," my old allied base. Incredible that he could be speaking to the enemy. Actually he was saying 'hello, hello.' Ridiculous of course, but that was what I believed for a moment.

Kokopo was an area on the coast of St. George Channel that reportedly was a haven of bountiful gardens lined with fruit trees--a land of plenty. We cherished the occasional false rumor that we might soon be moved to Kokopo and never be hungry again.

The Japanese word for natural gaseous crepitation was Kopopo. Joe Nason was asleep one afternoon when a particularly hostile guard was on duty and overhead loud crepitation in the prison cell. Angered by the annoyance, he raced into the cell shouting, "Dati da Kopopo?" Who? Nason woke up and asked what all the shouting was about, whereupon we told Joe that the guard wanted to know if anyone wanted to be moved to Kokopo. Joe eagerly volunteered by raising his hand and caught the wrath of the guards bamboo pole several times across his back. Joe wasn't particularly adept at the Jap language and amusingly gave it a slight boarding school French accent. His health was also usually poorer than most of us. It still surprises me that he was one of the seven American survivors at war's end. He was severely despondent on many occasions and would sometimes sit for hour upon hour in a prenatal position with the old horse blanket pulled up over his head and knees. A fraternal instinct among the rest of us compelled us to try to involve Joe in some activity that would snap him out of this semi-comatose attitude--all to no avail. He couldn't be aroused.

Once when the guards became inquisitive about Joe's withdrawn and immobile position under the blanket, we replied the Joe was attempting to cover up very unnatural acts and they should take measures to stop it. Like a volcano Joe threw off the blanket with wild cursing and protesting; threatening to murder each and every one of us. He nevertheless joined the world again and proceeded to hang onto life like the rest of us.

Back into the depression he went a month or so later; his arms clasped around his knees and pulled up into his chest and under his chin with the old blanket covering all. No response from him for days. A conspiracy arose to meet the situation. Holguin said, "I have a yard and a half of natural gas. What am I offered for it?" The price was about two dozen grains of rice and the delivery point was under Nason's blanket. Hell hath no fury like Nason's metamorphosis, but again he was delivered out of limbo; but not very thankful for the method of deliverance.

His own dignity and reverence brought him out of it from time to time when the rest of us would irreverently fake the voice of deceased prisoner by imploring to a blanket covered and withdrawn Nason that he "come on ooovveerr to the valley of death, there's plenty to eat over here and we're expecting you soooon." He called us 21 carat disrespectful bastards, sacrilegious and blasphemous infidels, but now he was again alive and warm bodied.

Depression was far from an unnatural occurrence. There were many forms to it and, it manifest itself in various ways. Over optimism, a special form, sometimes evolved from a choice rumor and the symptoms were easy to spot. A guy could talk to a guard who was somewhat depressed himself and deduce that Japan was ready to surrender tomorrow. He would go on a conversational jag for days telling everyone how convinced he was that our POW days were coming to an end. Ishimura had said this, or Ishimura had said that; all of which added up to a quick surrender. It was all fantasizing, whistling in the grave yard and the others knew it. They also knew it was a form of depression--one of the better forms; albeit until the let down came. Then the mercurial roller-coaster--the pit of despair--alternately, a bright sunny day could bring an extra cup of soup, or an interesting native prisoner could join us for a few days, or a rare compassionate guard could reassure us that we somehow had the strength to survive. Hold on, boys, nothing lasts forever. If we an go this far, we can go a little further. Think about those lucky guys up there right now bombing us just 15,000 feet above us--just three miles from where we're sitting. Remember, those vitamin chocolate bars and those sandwiches and that tea we carried on raids? Remember that enormous relief on the way home from a successful mission and the sure knowledge that a bottle of booze and a good nights sleep was at the end of the runway? Those lucky bastards; but we'll see it again some day. The rain on the tin roof is so loud now that the only thing to do is to stretch out, curl up on that old cotton blanket and dream, dream, dream. The magic carpet to another world and one more night to put behind us.

**Japanese atrocity**
(Photo courtesy Australian Memorial)

STANDARD TIME INDICATED
RECEIVED AT

*Postal Telegraph*

Mackay Radio     All America Cables
Commercial Cables     Canadian Pacific Telegraphs

THIS IS A FULL RATE TELEGRAM, CABLE-
GRAM OR RADIOGRAM UNLESS OTHERWISE
INDICATED BY SYMBOL IN THE PREAMBLE
OR IN THE ADDRESS OF THE MESSAGE.
SYMBOLS DESIGNATING SERVICE SELECTED
ARE OUTLINED IN THE COMPANY'S TARIFFS
ON HAND AT EACH OFFICE AND ON FILE WITH
REGULATORY AUTHORITIES.

TELEPHONE YOUR TELEGRAMS
TO POSTAL TELEGRAPH

Form 11

Q961  377 (TWO)  49 GOVT= PWMU WASHINGTON DC 7 6-17P= PM 6 16

J H MCMURRIA=
        933 BENNING BLVD (COLUMBUS GA)=

: THE SECRETARY OF AR E= OF WAR DESIRES ME TO EXPRESS HIS
DEEP REGRET THAT THE COMMANDING GENERAL UNITEDSTATES ARMY
FORCES IN SOUTHWEST PACIDIC AREA HAS REPOTED YOUR SON FIRST
LIEUTENATN JAMES A MCMURRIA AIR CORPS MISSING IN ACTION
SINCE JANUARY 20 PERIOD ADDITIONAL INFOGMATION WILL BE SENT
YOU WHEN RECEIVED=
        ULIO THE ADJUTANT GENERAL

CLASS OF SERVICE

This is a full-rate
Telegram or Cable-
gram unless its de-
ferred character is in-
dicated by a suitable
symbol above or pre-
ceding the address.

**WESTERN UNION**

A. N. WILLIAMS
PRESIDENT

(50)

SYMBOLS
DL = Day Letter
NL = Night Letter
LC = Deferred Cable
NLT = Cable Night Letter
Ship Radiogram

The filing time shown in the date line on telegrams and day letters is STANDARD TIME at point of origin. Time of receipt is STANDARD TIME at point of destination

QA19
WB170 54 GOVT=WUX WASHINGTON DC 5 442P                    1944 JAN 5 PM 3

MR MACMURRA=
        CARE OF MACMURRA MOTOR CO COLUMBUS GA=

THE NAME OF LT. JAMES A MACMURRA HAS BEEN MENTIONED IN AN
ENEMY BROADCAST AS A PRISONER IN JAPANESE HANDS. THE PURPOSE
OF SUCH BROADCASTS IS TO GAIN LISTENERS FOR THE ENEMY
PROPAGANDA WHICH THEY CONTAIN: BUT THE ARMY IS CHECKING THE
ACCURACY OF THIS INFORMATION AND WILL ADVISE YOU AS SOON
AS POSSIBLE=
        FOREIGN BROADCAST INTELLIGENCE SERVICE OF FEDERAL
        COMMUNICATIONS COMMISSION.

THE COMPANY WILL APPRECIATE SUGGESTIONS FROM ITS PATRONS CONCERNING ITS SERVICE

# Chapter 20

Hasigowa, "the Farmer," came on duty in the early morning of April 12, 1945. An utterly complacent guy, he reflected the simple calm and emotional stability that we imagined his rural, uneventful upbringing had inculcated. I think the Japanese call it Carmi--what will be, will be. In the tone of voice and with the lack of enthusiasm that one would say "It looks like rain today," Hasigowa placidly announced "Americano number one captain, die finish." President Roosevelt is dead. Silence. What does it mean? We were dumbfounded. How will this affect us, the war? Who will be the new president? We were told the "new captain's" name was Tolmon. Anybody ever heard of Tolmon? Even after we remember the difficulty Japanese had in pronouncing an "R," we never heard of a Truman. Before the day was over, however, the Jap propaganda machine was working and brought us visitors that claimed Roosevelt's successor was a pacifist, a weakling and would capitulate to Japanese demands. They said Tolman was at odds with Makasa and that the Nippon flag would soon be flying over Washington. This sad news came to us at a particularly bad time. Beri-beri, scurvy, and malaria had taken a heavy toll in prisoner deaths during the early months of 1945. The number of prisoners, which was at one time as high at 76, was not reduced to about ten. It is a rather odd fact to remember that of those ten survivors, most of them had been shot down and captured early in the war and, from point of time in service, had been compounded the longest. I suppose to some extent it was a matter of adjusting or not being able to adjust--Occidental Carmi--and above all, a strong will to live. But with Roosevelt dead and with a weak successor, what was the use of struggling. Our fanatical captors had many times told us that Japan was prepared to fight for a hundred years. They certainly were preserving the local food supply as though they believed it might just last that long.

Several things, nevertheless, fortified us against believing this new rash of propaganda. One was the sad death of Charlie Lanphier. Charlie's health deteriorated after capture along the line of so many others--rapid loss of weight accompanied by malaria and debilitation of body and spirit. Charlie wanted to survive but couldn't gather the strength. We had become warm friends and enjoyed each other greatly. A close companionship with him grew rapidly during the months I knew him.

Early one evening after he had been seized with an unusually violent bout of malaria, coupled with massive edema, it looked as though he wasn't going to make it. He crawled over to the Benjo bucket to relive his rampant dysentery but was unable to get off his knees. He fell into my arms and with somewhat labored breathing began to whisper. He apologized for his condition and assured me that with only a milkshake or a fresh salad he could easily go on. However, he felt his time had come and that before going he wanted to tell me a great secret. In the faintest voice, he said that he had a brother named Tommy who was a P-38 fighter pilot and that Tommy was credited with shooting down the famous Admiral Yamamoto on Bouganville, just prior to Charlie's capture. Charlie hadn't told anyone of this, including his fellow prisoners, until now for fear of reprisals if word should get out to the Japs. He died quietly in his sleep that night.

Less than a month later, Japanese naval personnel wandered into our area. Apparently they had an afternoon off duty and curiosity and boredom prompted them to visit the area where we were imprisoned. Surprisingly, the Kempe Tai allowed them to converse with us directly and without censure. In "ligua franca" we bluffed our way with them to the extent that they admitted that Germany had surrendered to the Allies. They were adamant, however, in the belief that Japan could and would go it alone to a victorious end.

One group of downed fliers that was brought in several months earlier included a guy named Boynton--Pappy Boynton. I think Pappy was fished out of Blanche Bay right in Rabaul Harbor and turned over to the Kempe Tai, who had two or three other prisoners in tow at the time. They were brought straight to our cells except that Pappy, ace that he was with over 30 victories, got special attention with regards to interrogation and wasn't put in with us. The Kempe Tai kept Pappy in a private cell across the street from us in the old frame, two-story building; a portion of which was a brothel. This was prior to the March '44 devastation of downtown. The guys that did join us, however, told us a great deal about

Pappy's exploits, and we were disappointed that we didn't' get any exposure to him. From all subsequent accounts, Pappy wasn't kept in Rabaul for very long. Somehow the Japs got him out of there and up to Japan. I'm sure he would have been a great morale booster had we been able to talk to him. For his sake, however, I'm sure he was better off getting up to the mother country rather than being kept in Fortress Rabaul--the now crumbling tower of strength in the Southwest Pacific.

Since the war, a TV series names "Ba-Ba Black Sheep" was made around Pappy's exploits, and I enjoyed it immensely; although its flavor was a tad more theatrical than the real thing.

**Cadet James A. McMurria, Army Air Corps Flight School, Randolph Field, San Antonio, Texas, 1941.**

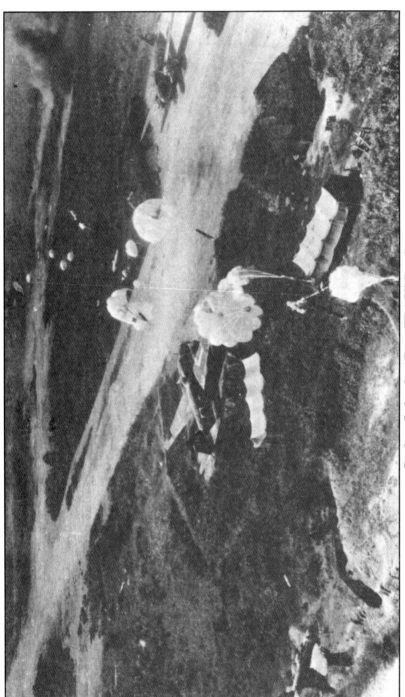

Back to Rabaul – "Para FRAG" Bombs

# Chapter 21

The first experience one has of witnessing a formation of heavy bombers attacking your area accompanied by the massive swooshing sound of a train of bombs falling in your direction is a frightening thing. Under good conditions the bombs themselves could be seen falling through the air leaving little doubt in your mind that you are the ultimate target. A sense of helplessness envelopes you. In the final moments of agonizing frustration, however, and with great relief, one realizes that the actual target area could be miles away. The relief diminishes in direct proportion to the proximity of the target. After hundreds of such experiences, our proficiency in dimensional calculation became so sensitive that we became slightly blase'. Such was our case after a couple of years of watching 17's and 24's unleashing their devastation on Rabaul. As flight after flight of heavies assaulted our area, our practiced eye prompted us to blithely say on occasions, "Well, we don't have to worry about those guys, they're after the harbor (a mile away) or they're after Lakunai airdrome (3 miles away). Knowing the ineptitude of some bombardiers it's strange that we took this attitude, but mostly we were right. If allied bombs hit miles away from our area, we jokingly attributed the drop to a group to which some prisoner formerly belonged. "That must have been your bunch of amateurs, tonight," or "When will the 321st squadron ever become effective; you would think they would have improved somewhat now that you're not in there with them to screw it up."

An aura of sophistication grew among the prisoners, whereby we could quickly estimate the altitude, the attitude and the flight path of allied raids, to the extent that with a casual bored yawn we announced to each other, "No need to take shelter (if in fact it was available), those B-24 jerks will miss us by hundreds of yards." Sometimes the decibels created by a large formation salvoing 1,000 ponders was so low (high) that there was no noise at all, just an earth quaking vibration that was even more shattering than the noise that usually followed smaller or individual drops.

Para-frag raids on our area were less frequent but no less effective. Low level strafing by fighter's didn't give you time for anxiety. But pseudo sophistication still prevailed. Once in a quick flash of terror, a P-38 riddled our area without warning--catching guards and prisoners alike, unaware. A 50-caliber bullet pierced the corrugated roof of our cell and penetrated the floor just inches from my ear, while I was reclining and smoking a forbidden handmade cigarette. With nonchalance, I flipped the ashes over my shoulder into the newly created receptacle made by the bullet and remarked, "How convenient, my own personal ash tray."

Allied fighters on a low level strafing raid almost always caught us by surprise and I believe they were very effective and dreaded by everyone.

I mentioned rolling rope for the Japanese. This activity was determined to be a suitable occupation for emaciated POW's not having the strength required for heavier work. Actually, the project was a face saving swap-off for our captors. During a period when our death rate from starvation and disease was usually high, we sent a formal message to Kempe Tai headquarters that we would prefer execution rather than slow starvation. The message was received with indignation. Japanese Bushido (Chivalry) would hardly sanction such incivility. However, if we wanted more food we would have to become more productive. Thus the rope-rolling program was born and to our great relief since our request for execution was not without some degree of bluff. The improved menu included, in addition to our rice ball, one stalk of bananas each week for three weeks then the matter was dropped; but the rope-rolling continued.

The production method for a very low quality, low tensile strength rope was as follows:

Two pieces of coconut husk, having been rolled by hand into roughly the shape of a long cigar, were pinioned to the floor by the big toe. Similar pieces of husk partially matted into the first husk but extending several inches above the original, were rolled between the two palms of the hands and given a right hand twist. Additional pieces were then added and twisted to the other ply, also with a right hand twist, thus producing a loose two-ply rope. After several feet were produced, the two plies were tightened up by giving the finished product a left-hand twist. We never saw the practical application of our rope, but the prisoners must have rolled several miles of it. From our own standpoint we found it to be a cigarette lighter far superior to the cotton thread that previously hung smoldering in our small bomb shelter.

During the most of our confinement the only clothing we wore was a "Fundushe." This is a strip of cloth about 12 inches wide to which a string was sewn at each of the two corners. The Fundishee was about 36 inches long. The cloth was held behind you and the two strings were brought around the waist and tied in front, then the cloth dangling behind was brought up between the legs and tucked under the string around the waist. The edges were seamed and unfortunately were the favorite hiding place for lice. Many hours of the day were spent seeking out those illusive lice and killing them. Eradicating them entirely was an impossible job, but since I don't recall them biting to any unbearable degree, they provided a past-time not altogether boring. As a matter of fact a sort of competition developed to see who could kill the most lice within a given time.

During my first year I was allowed to take one bath, consisting of standing out in the rain without any soap. Sometime, during my second year we made a rather strong protest that we should be given soap and water for a first class bath. We were refused the request because of a lack of water. There was an oil drum outside our cell for the purpose of catching rain off the roof but for a sustained period we had had no rain and the drum was empty. The guards agreed, however, that if water was available, they would allow us to use it for a bath. Of course they could have provided water from elsewhere but that was too much trouble. They would give us no SARVIS, their word for service or gift.

Some of the more devout Catholics among us had taught the group the three holy mysteries: the Joyful; the Sorrowful and the Glorious. We learned the five tenets that accompanied each of the mysteries and said the Hail Marys while reflecting on them. We also learned the meaning of a Novena. When the guards refused to allow us to bathe because of a lack of water in the drum, we announced that we would call for Divine intervention and pray for

rain. A Novena was instituted and miraculously within a few days
we had rain and a 55-gallon drum full of fresh rain water. Our
comment to the guards that this was "Christo Sarvis" made, I think,
an indelible impression, and we were let outside to revel in the
glorious and heavenly provided H20 and a bar of homemade
coconut soap. The guards were not the only ones duly impressed
and we thanked the Almighty for, not only the water, but for the
blessing of Christianity and its profound lesson to the Japanese.

I don't believe that lice carried any disease or was the basis of
our serious illness. The mosquito was responsible for rampant
malaria, and malnutrition brought on the rest: beri-beri, scurvy
and general debilitation. The most common manifestation of this
was edema. This, as I understand it, is a result of a breaking down
of the blood chemistry. Insufficient nitrogen or some other element
in the blood, impedes the circulatory system in some way so that
swelling develops in that part of the body most distant from the
heart. Pregnant women standing on their feet for a long period
develop swollen ankles. In a reclining position, the heart has less
of a pumping problem because of gravity. Month after month, year
after year, edema haunted the prisoners. Skin and bones was the
norm, but the addition of edema to the physique caused an
unhealthy puffiness giving a 90 pound skeleton the appearance of
a flabby welter weight; that is, when he was in a reclining position.
If the body sat upright, gravity caused the broken down blood
serum to collect in the lower extremities. After a night's sleep,
prone, the excess serum would be evenly distributed over the body,
and the ungodly appearance of a so swollen face, that the eyes were
mere slits, was devastating. Huge ankles, obese thighs, puffy
fingers, quart sized scrotums, wasted buttocks now unhealthily
restored to size by an accumulation of serum was heart-rending.
The skin on my lower legs was peeled and raw. The outer skin and
hair long gone; morning would present me with a wet pool of excess
uncirculated serum on the floor. The hideous smile of a still
hopeful prisoner, swollen with edema, was the gory height of
optimism. "Our friends are in the Philippines now and it will soon
be over. Maybe they'll give us more rice tomorrow, and did you
notice the soup had more topping yesterday? If they have sustained
us this far, surely they want us to survive, if for no other reason,
they belong to the world of humanity and need at least a semblance

of evidence of that fact." Every surviving day became a victory. Every survivor became tangible evidence in their minds that Bushido still existed, a mighty difference of interpretation, a product of two worlds of environment. From the standpoint of quality of life, we were the losers. But as the war went northward, we were the winners, if we could but hold on.

In the back of everyone's mind, although it was seldom voiced, was the dull ache caused by the realization that our loved ones back home were grieving. Most had no way of knowing that we were still alive. The standard military telegram to families back home, in such circumstances, was a curt notice that your relative was "missing in action and presumed dead after being shot down by enemy forces in the vicinity of such and such an island."

In the form of a cruel hoax, I presumed, the Japanese announced one day that I would be allowed to write a letter to my parents. We were being antagonized unmercifully at the time, and naturally I thought this was a joke, another item to be held up and ridiculed. I couldn't take the gamble so I accepted the questionable opportunity by writing a calm letter filled with lies about my condition as a POW, I was told that the letter would be sent to a free port in Africa and thence forwarded to America. I learned later that instead, the letter wound up in the hands of Tokyo Rose who broadcasted it over short wave radio. Patriotic and neutral citizens all over the world, on their own, monitored these broadcasts and in the summer of 1944, my family received letters from a woman in India, a Canadian and from others; saying that they had intercepted a Tokyo Rose transmission that mentioned my being held captive by the Japanese.

My family was tremendously thankful for this kindness and took courage from it. However, the military also monitored the program and shortly thereafter a message arrived from the army saying that such broadcasts were not to be trusted and implied that their purpose was largely enemy propaganda. Of course, I knew nothing of this and felt throughout the war that my parents and friends were completely without information about me and doubtlessly considered me dead.

WESTERN UNION

CLASS OF SERVICE

This is a full-rate Telegram or Cable-gram unless its de-ferred character is in-dicated by a suitable symbol above or pre-ceding the address.

BM121

A. N. WILLIAMS
PRESIDENT

NEWCOMB CARLTON
CHAIRMAN OF THE BOARD

J. C. WILLEVER
FIRST VICE-PRESIDENT

1220

SYMBOLS

DL = Day Letter
NT = Overnight Telegram
LC = Deferred Cable
NLT = Cable Night Letter
Ship Radiogram

The filing time shown in the date line on telegrams and day letters is STANDARD TIME at point of origin. Time of receipt is STANDARD TIME at point of destination

LA238W (EIGHT) GOVT NL=PXXWMUB.WASHINGTON DC 20

MR AND MRS JOHN H MCMURRA=

933 (BENNING) BLVD COLUMBUS GA=

FOLLOWING SHORT WAVE BROADCAST FROM JAPAN HAS BEEN
INTERCEPTED" QUOTE-EARL DEAR FOLKS I HAVE NEVER TOLD YOU A
LIE INTENTIONALLY ABOUT ANYTHING THAT MATTERED. I WONT NOW
WELL, IVE BEEN CAPTURED BY THE JAPANESE AND I KNOW YOUR FIRST
THOUGHTS, PLEASE DONT WORRY, I AM WELL TREATED AND MY ONLY
DISCOMFORT IS BECOMING USED TO JAPANESE FOOD, ILL BE HOME
AFTER THIS MESS IS OVER AND LOVE ONLY FOR THAT DAY, NOTIFY
FRIENDS, A LETTER TO MARY FRANCES (SMITH?) TEN WOODLAWN
WESTA (GREENVILLE) SOUTHCAROLINA, I HAVE A RECEIPT FOR 360
ODD DOLLARS FROM THE COMMONWEALTH BANK OF AUSTRALIA IN BILL
FOLD, ASK (STOKES?) IF HE RECEIVED THE MONEY TO MY ACCOUNT, MY
HEALTH IS GOOD, MY HEART IS HEAVY UNTIL I SEE YOU AGAIN, DONT
WEAR MY CLOTHES OUT AND WATCH OUT FOR MY FINANCES, INQUIRE AT
THE RED CROSS FOR FURTHER COMMUNICATION, THE MOST BEST LOVE IN
THE WORLD TO YOU ALL JAMES A MCMURRA, UNQUOTE-AS THIS BROADCAST
IS ENEMY PROPAGANDA IT CANNOT BE ACCEPTED AS OFFICIAL REPORT
FOR WAR DEPARTMENT, STOP, LETTER FOLLOWS=

GUILLION PROVOST MARSHAL GENERAL

360.

THE COMPANY WILL APPRECIATE SUGGESTIONS FROM ITS PATRONS CONCERNING ITS SERVICE

# Chapter 22

As the languid summer of 1945 approached and military activity droned down to a slow pace, there were just nine survivors in the camp: Escoe Palmer, Joe Holguin, Al Quinones, Joe Nason, Bob Keptia, John Murphy, Dick Lannigan, Donald Atkiss and myself. All had withstood the rigors of serious illness without medical attention plus unmerciful starvation. To some extent the Japanese respected us for our stamina. It would be unfair not to mention, however, that the enemy had also suffered disease, particularly malaria. Atabrin was a relatively new drug at that time and I'm sure there was none of it in Rabaul. Quinine was their only protection, and it was far less efficacious. Their meager supply of quinine, their word for it was "inki," was certainly not to be wasted on prisoners of war.

An inquisitive and inquiring Dr. Hirano appeared at our compound in July of 1945. He spoke passable English, having, as he said, attended medical seminars in America prior to the war. Even in our debilitated and mentally lethargic condition, the nine of us immediately agreed among ourselves that Hirano was not to be trusted. In an ingratiating manner, he recalled the humanitarian efforts of medical giants like Leuenhouk and Swietzer, Cure and Pasteur. "Spacey" is a currently popular word unknown at that time, but Hirano was "spacey". With no medical attention whatsoever, the nine prisoners he was attempting to seduce, had conquered malaria. His question was, "Are Occidentals more immune to malaria than Orientals?" In his crude laboratory, he suggested he would like to study the relative blood make up of the two groups. I felt that in my own case, having suffered numerous sieges of malaria and now being free of it, that I had built up a natural immunity just as most New Guinea natives had done.

Dr. Hirano selected five of the nine prisoners who were free of malaria and proceeded to inject us with it. He promised medical attention and supervision along with his experiment. We immediately came down with malaria. Many blood samples were taken from us for his examination and experimentation. The injections were given on July 15, 1945. No medical attention was forthcoming. On August 1st Donald Atkins and Dick Lannigan were dead. The war was over two weeks later. Hirano was scheduled to be tried by the War Crimes Commission after their surrender, but he cut his own throat with a razor blade and died without ever being tried.

Time and time again in the spring and summer of 1945, we noticed small groups of Japanese clustered together in serious conversation and in hushed tones, just out of earshot. It was a great boost for us to occasionally decipher a word like Manilla or Okinawa in context with B-ne ju ku (B-29). There was a marked dimunition of their arrogance and disdain for us. Delightful evidence of this was the gift of one volume of an encyclopedia one day in early June, 1945. The subject covered Humbolt through Matla, Vol. 5. This was the first reading material I had seen in over 2-1/2 years. How we devoured it! It had been published in England in the 19th century and was totally out of date, but such a sensation to consume every word! Each of the nine of us read every word of it. We drew straws for reading priority. Some of the guards resented the gesture, but the consensus was with us.

The next surprising magnanimity was the appearance of an ancient Singer sewing machine that had been brought to Rabaul from the Philippines. It was in poor repair, but the ingenious Joe Holguin guaranteed to fix it, and fix it he did. He then quickly learned to operate it; and as the word spread, Joe was in great demand as an amateur tailor. He repaired their uniforms and any other item of cloth needing attention. I think Joe even fixed a few pairs of their shoes. Attitudes this late in the war had changed to the slight extent that Joe was not ordered to do this mending,but pleasantly requested to do so and was often courteously thanked for his efforts.

By this time the prisoners had inherited a threadbare pair of pants and shirts that had been cast off by some solider. The material was about the weight of pajama cloth, but was entirely satisfactory due to the rather warm climate of Rabaul. There was only a slight seasonal variation in temperature, and the nights were often very pleasant.

Time dragged on with endless abandon marked only now by

more frequent rumors based largely on speculation that peace and deliverance could be imminent. Then came the tragic Hirano experience. The death of Don Atkins and Dick Lannigan on August 1, 1945 devastated our thin optimism. With only seven emaciated prisoners left out of seventy-six, what incentive would our captors have in delivering this motley group to the victorious Allies. We wondered what new medical experiments might be performed on us. Perhaps this might be their method of extermination, which would provide no evidence of the conditions under which we had lived. Extreme anxiety gripped us for two weeks following Don and Dick's untimely demise. Two weeks brought us to August 14th, that happy day!

Tsukihara went on duty at mid-morning on the 14th, bringing with him an armful of clothing, consisting of some rather decent looking shirts and trousers. He presented them to us and with great flourish announced, "I am removing this lock from the prison door and throwing it away, and the kind commander has agreed that you may come outside anytime you wish. You are not to leave this small area, however, without supervision. There is a possibility that you may be allowed to plant a garden and grow your own food. Bathe and burn your old clothing, and change to these nice uniforms." The impact of this statement was perplexing. Surely something tremendous was going on, and we went into a fit of uncontrollable optimism; but what was that about a garden? If the war was over, why plant a garden. A garden requires months to fruition. The next statement really peaked our imagination. Tsukihara said, "Tomorrow morning, the Tisa (Colonel) wants to speak to you personally." I suppose that over the nearly three years that I had been imprisoned, I had only seen the Tisa on two or three occasions, and then only at a distance as he strolled majestically through a nearby papaya and cassava grove. He presented an image of ultimate dignity and serenity with his proud Samurai sword and polished boots strolling ethereally through the grove alone. His command held him in great awe and reverence, and tomorrow he was going to speak to us! Sleep came easy that night after being out in the sunshine and fresh air most of the day, but not without deep discussions among us as to what it all meant.

Morning arrived with much hustle and bustle among the

158 Fight for Survival

guards preparing the area for a visit from the Colonel. The cell
floor was washed and scrubbed by both prisoners and guards. The
ground was swept and the guard box was manicured until
everything was immaculate. The Colonel arrived ceremoniously
and requested the seven prisoners to be seated on the ground in
front of the position he had taken standing at attention. We bowed
very politely to him, and he return the courtesy in kind. The guards
were asked to retire from the area leaving him alone with us except
for an official interpreter and a large box placed on the ground by
his side. His carefully selected words amounted roughly to the
following:

"Peaceful agreements between Japan and the Allies are being
concluded by the supreme commanders. Hostilities have come to
an end between our nations. A peace now exists largely because
of the infliction of a most extraordinary weapon upon Japan. No
human being or plant life will be possible in the area exposed to
the weapon for the next seventy-five years. The nature of the
weapon was unknown to him, but in the interest of humanity
(strange word) the combatants mutually agree that there should be
a cessation of all hostilities." No mention of surrender. His
inflections and vague choice of words left little doubt in our minds
as to the real situation. He then opened the box next to him and
presented each of the seven of us with a bottle of whiskey, a bottle
of wine, a large bag of hardtack, a small can of milk, a fig bar and
a bar of chocolate. He told us that this ration was the identical
ration that the Army and the Navy was prepared to issued each
Japanese soldier and sailor and airman as a final ration in the event
that Rabaul was invaded by the Allies. He expressed no pleasure
that this did not happen. He then told us that he had issued orders
for us to be removed from this area to a more pleasant environment
up in the mountains, a place called Nanga Nanga, within the next
few days. With that he bowed and retired, a still proud but
defeated old soldier. We strangely shared his pathos as we had
known something of defeat ourselves. His life was over, but ours
was being renewed.

We enjoyed the food profoundly. We shared the whiskey with
the guards, the most enigmatic drinking companions. Drunk and
dazed by the momentous events of the day, we set fire to the cell

with the help of the guards, after removing our possessions, consisting of a cup, blanket, playing cards and an encyclopedia. We dug up scores of cassava roots and roasted them in the fire. We feasted on luscious, ripe papayas from the grove and after the festive orgy, we fell into a drunken sleep for the remaining few hours of the night, to arise like a Phoenix when the new morning arrived.

A bright sun awakened a badly hung over group from our open air pallets about 9 A.M. No guards were in sight for an hour, until Yamashita showed up with a full bucket of hot Mesu Shiru (bean curd soup) swimming with tiny fish, and a hugh bucket of steaming rice. His demeanor was still inscrutable, but, on the whole, I believe he enjoyed seeing us consume the fare. Other guards arrived and made an effort to be pleasant. I believe they were in as much of a quandary as we were as victors. We still had no protection and in a fit of savage revenge, we still could be murdered; yet I believe they were under orders to continue their vigilance, and thank God for Japanese military discipline. Nearby, disgruntled troops were a definite threat to our safety. As a thoroughly dilapidated truck arrived after breakfast to take us up a mountain to Nanga Nanga, Yamashita confided to us that we would be passing through various concentrations of troops and that the reaction of these troops was unknown to them, and that they were taking great precaution to safely escort us to our new station. The seven of us and seven heavily armed guards began the 15 mile trip winding around steep cliffs and gullies, through devastated areas of bombed out equipment and gun emplacements. Musty caves and revetments were everywhere. The Japs had truly gone underground. Life had become untenable on the surface; a thoroughly unpleasant existence for them, and all the more basis for their animosity for the surviving POW's.

Passing out of a heavily wooded area and into a broad clearing the truck entered the encampment of a group of Imperial Marines; the so-called elite Japanese warriors. Our guards steeled themselves for the encounter. Our driver pulled the truck to an abrupt halt and, not being a member of the Kempe Tai, dismounted and slowly walked away from the scene. A heated confrontation developed between our Gunso and the irate commander of the garrison. The shouting match between them was so fast and furious that we were unable to understand the language, but the drift of it was loud and clear. We were ordered to dismount, and those of us that were able stood at attention. Nason and Kepchia were obliged to assume a reclining position due to weakness. The sabre-rattling conversation, laced with threats and menacing fingers pointed at us, lasted for about 10 minutes before big Yamashita Gunso prevailed and, though still under protest, we were allowed to continue.

The outside world, aside from the devastation, was wondrous to behold. The blue sky, the coconut plantations, the green tropical foliage and the aquamarine water of the harbor now below us, was exhilarating. The world with all its beauty was still out there waiting for us. Reaching a higher elevation it became even more beautiful as Nanga Nanga plantation spread out wondrously before our eyes.

Under a canopy of huge ironwood trees bordered by lush tropical growth, a gazebo had been erected as our living quarters. It would not do credit to the formal garden of Buckingham Palace, but for us it was heaven to behold. The gazebo had an open air platform with a pitched roof, not requiring screens or even netting since mosquitoes were not a problem up there. The air was cool and light. The aroma of the foliage, sphagnum and apple moss provided by mother nature humbled us into reverent thanksgiving. Hibiscus, d'albertis, flame trees and frangipani were everywhere.

Some sort of headquarters detachment had previously been stationed in this area and there were numerous field grade officers and enlisted men in the cadre. A detachment of Kempe Tai also lived in the area and as we arrived at the gazebo, an orderly appeared with hot tea served in tin cups. Another orderly presented us with an envelope filled with inki and vitamin tablets. We refreshed ourselves with a quick snooze on top of fresh cotton blankets in the gorgeous mountain air. At noon time we were given as much rice as would recently have been served us for a week, along with a hot soup containing a few carrots, cabbage leaves and some delicious sliced skimono (cucumbers); nourishment for the mind as much as the body. Our stomachs were full for the first time in captivity, but our appetite was not abated. Within an hour after lunch Ishimura thrust a gallon can of tomato jam into our platform. After dividing it precisely into seven wooden bowls, we consumed it in a matter of minutes and then smilingly relaxed again into the arms of Morpheus. Abundantly refreshed by the nap, we tried our legs and wandered wondrously for several hundred yards around the camp before being offered a barrel of fresh bath water. We then dressed and shaved with a pair of good scissors and received three nattily dressed Japanese officers, a major and two captains. I don't remember their names, but they were solicitous and came bearing three small cans of salmon which they shared with us; everyone using his personal chopsticks and passing the cans back and forth. The extent of their conversation evolved mostly around where we were from, our former occupation and our families back home; delicately avoiding any controversial subjects.

The next morning a real emotional breakdown occurred among us as a result of an ancient phonograph being brought over to us. Two thick victrola records came with the machine. There were recordings on both sides of the record. Richard Talber, the famous German tenor, sang "Humoresque" on one side and an enchanting string quartet played Saint-Saens's "The Swan" from the French opera "Les Animals" on the other. Tears rolled unashamedly from our eyes. Uncontrollable emotion lapsed into deep meditation and not a word was spoken for hours as we played the music over and over re-encountering Eastern culture after an Oriental nightmare.

I failed to mention that just prior to leaving our last camp, another prisoner was brought in. His name as Ronnie Warren, a pilot from Christ Church, New Zealand. The Anzanks, by then had become the exclusive guardians of the enemy forces trapped in Northern New Britain and New Ireland, with the exception of a few American forces mostly stationed at Finshafen, New Guinea. The Anzaks continued to raid Rabaul occasionally and Ronnie was a late and unfortunate casualty. He was shot down by anti-aircraft fire and in the process suffered a broken leg. A doctor had attempted to set the fracture and had given him a crude splint, but all in all Ronnie didn't suffer too much and was a magnificent boost to our spirits with his fresh account of the tremendous victories the Allies had gained. His total time as a POW was only about three weeks.

Soon after reaching our camp at Nanga Nanga I was allowed to have a pencil and paper. Thirty-three months before, January 19, 1943, I had entered my last account in a diary that I had been keeping. Today, September 2, 1945, I joyously picked up a pencil and resumed my efforts. From the worn and faded copy which I still have in my possession I recount the following script:

September 2, 1945--The wind blew and the gossip flew all last night. We can see the water below from up here and the mountains that enclose it. Matsuta Chosa (Major) put us straight as to our position there in a short talk. We are to be gentlemen again, and we find it delightful to accept such ingratiation and freedom. I'm still very swollen with edema and tropical ulcers, but it can't be long now. The newcomer, Ronnie Warren, is full of pep and cheers us up tremendously. He was in the States just a year ago--trained in Calgary, Alberta. He says somebody named Frank Sinatra is all the rage there.

September 3, 1945--Figured it up and breakfast this morning concludes my 2973rd consecutive meal of rice. There are rumors of butter for lunch. Imagine!

September 4, 1945--Slept well last night. Plenty of wind up here--reminds me of October back home. I now possess a spoon which Fuji gave me. No more eating with hashes. Quinones has found some coffee and is now preparing it on an open fire. Its time for the new guards and its going to be Ishimura, Matsuoka and Tokada. Think I'll walk down to the point and look at the harbor, maybe that beautiful boat will show up today. This afternoon we were given a salary for the first time. My pay was 85 yen a month minus 27 yen for food. However, during the first seven months I was a prisoner, I paid 60 yen a month for food. The doctor visited again and gave us some vitamin power and said we could get two cans of either salmon or corned beef per day for the group.

September 5, 1945--Hottest rumor today is just three more days here and we'll be out. Big conference in Tokyo. Wish I could quit worrying about it and just eat and sleep like Murphy does.

Someone just offered 20 yen for a quarter of a can of corned beef. Believe I'll keep my quarter of can. I have promised to send Murph some pecans and a recipe for pecan pie, a Roget's Thesaurus and a copy of Service's "Spell of the Yukon." He is to send me his Pidgin English dictionary, a copy of "Around the Boree Log" by Father John O'Brien and a Mt. Hargan ceremonial axe, a beautifully carved wood and stone weapon. The major visited again today and made it quite clear that the Japanese hate the Russians intensely. They apparently broke a treaty and entered the war against the Japs just before it was over. He says that the Japs will clean up the Russians anytime the U.S. will give them some ships and planes. Tomorrow should be full of revelations. Nason sat up with Hasigowa last night and extracted the information that a carrier took some Japanese aboard near here today, and that it will enter the harbor tomorrow. The Australians were informed of our presence and were disturbed over our small number.

September 6, 1945--Hard trying to sleep last night with so much anxiety. Dreamed about Mary Frances-can't put it all together--is she married? Couldn't blame her if she is. This is all like being born again. Had a full blown earthquake today. Everyone looked for a safe place where there were no trees falling. What an irony to die from an earthquake after all of this.

The following day was a paroxysm of emotional excitement. The sunlight and very air around us implied that "this was it." Day of days! There was an electrifying bustle about it and still no word. Then the word leaked, the ship was in the harbor; a mad crippled dash to he point overlooking Simpson Harbor, and there she was. A four stack destroyer lay idle in the calm water of Blanche Bay about 15 miles east of us. There was a tremendous amount of activity among the Japanese, and we were told to prepare to leave. We bathed as quickly as possible, scooped our few possessions, in my case the encyclopedia, my menus and a deck of cards made from Japanese cardboard cigarette packages; and fell in at attention before Major Matsuda. Joe Holguin recalled in a letter to me recently the following events and in his words said:

"About 10 A.M., September 7, 1945, Colonel Kikuchi, commander of the Kempe Tai battalion arrived at our camp with two staff cars and a flat bed truck. They were to transport us to the harbor where we were to be handled over to an Australian Navy destroyer. McMurria, Murphy, Quinones, Holguin and Warren boarded the flat bed and were joined by Lt. Kato. Nason, Palmer and Kepchia, who were too weak to stand, were placed in one of the staff cars. Col. Kukuchi, Maj. Natsuda and two other officers occupied the other car.

We pulled out of camp in a three car caravan with Col. Kikuchis's car leading and the truck bringing up the rear. In about five minutes we arrived at the headquarters of the Military Police--a row of thatched-roofed tropical barracks forming a semi-circle around a small parade ground. The Japanese flag was waving from a tall pole in front of the building area. The entire battalion had formed in front of the headquarters, in a class A uniform and the soldiers were at "parade rest," their rifles sparkling in the sun as we pulled up. At that instant, the whole battalion came to attention. The caravan stopped. Col. Kikuchi and his small staff stepped out of their car and joined the battalion. Lt. Kato stayed with us on the truck. The officer in charge then shouted "Kirei" (present arms). Every soldier brought his rifle forward to the salute position. For a brief moment we didn't know what to do. It had been so long since anyone had saluted us. Immediately, we returned the salute making sure we made individual salutes to the right, to the center and to the left. It was stretched out quite a ways from one end of the parade ground to the other.

When we had finished our salute, the battalion was then called to "port arms" and then to "present arms" again. We responded by returning their salute in the same way as before. Three times they saluted us, and three times we returned their salute and with a flourish we pulled slowly past our former captors and left their ranks forever as we headed down the mountain for the harbor."

Our worn out truck threatened several times to give up the effort and lie down and die in the middle of that narrow, pot marked trail taking us below. It's engine coughed and spit, it's brakes screeched and it's body groaned. For God's sake let's don't miss the boat now. Are they waiting for us at a dock or do they really know we're coming? The startling obeisance just show us on the parade ground momentarily obfuscated the memory of so many deaths from hunger and abuse. We blended our voices into an old song called "Wait for the Wagon" and unharmoniously shouted the last line --"and we'll all go home."

When we reached the shoreline our truck begrudgingly sputtered its way through a shallow slough and over a sharp rise that was almost its undoing and into a cleared area from which a pier extended 100 yards out into the harbor. Not a soul was in sight, but we had a much better view of the Australian destroyer anchored off shore. We could see the outlines of men aboard her. In unison we all exclaimed, "My God, they're a bunch of giants." That impression is indelibly etched in my mind. After living with the Japanese for so long we were appalled at the physical difference in the two races. The Aussie sailors looked enormous by comparison.

The five of us climbed down the truck while Nason, Palmer and Kepchia got out of the staff car. One of the officers and Lt. Kato remained with us while the rest of the Japanese contingent drove off in the direction of the town of Rabaul five or six miles to the west. Presently we heard the drone of another truck approaching from the opposite direction. As it pulled up and stopped we were amazed at seeing twenty-six British soldiers unloading in a very military manner. Their British uniforms were fairly in tact and their health, though not perfect, was vastly superior to ours. They fell in a rigid formation, their ranking officer, a sergeant called the roll, did a smart about face, and saluted the accompanying Japanese guard. They then broke ranks and promptly joined us for ravenous conversation.

They told us that they were the remnant of a battalion under General Percival that had surrendered to Gen. Yamashita in Singapore on February 15, 1942. I had been a prisoner longer than anyone in our group and these men had been captured nearly a year earlier than I. Most of them were Scots. We had a wonderful time mixing with them and swapping stories for a short while until our attention was drawn to the destroyer where a motor launch was being lowered. We could see several men in the launch as it sped up the harbor in our direction. Excitement among us was rampant but died out quickly as the launch sped right past our pier about a half mile out and continued on its way up the harbor toward the town. What now, dammit, are they going to pick us up? As we watched the launch we were diverted by the arrival of a staff car containing a couple of Japanese officers who flitted about inspecting the prisoners in an ingratiating manner. Suddenly a cheer arose as the launch reversed its course and headed directly toward us.

A two hundred pound, broad shouldered Royal Australian Navy Captain Morris climbed smartly out of the launch followed by his aide and a Japanese officer. He told us that he thought he had seen us prisoners as he passed by the first time, but that the stupid Jap officer with him had disagreed and insisted that we were further up the coast. He was very irritated over this delay and apologized for it. He then remarked that we sure looked hungry and asked us that we would like to eat. We agreed that we would like bread and butter and something to drink where upon he dispatched his aide to the destroyer while he negotiated with a pompous Jap officer with a crudely constructed peg leg. By the time Capt. Morris had signed appropriate papers, the launch returned with two wash tubs full of bread and butter and some Australian sasparilla. We consumed this in about five minutes and were then offered a cigarette from a white package of Lucky Strikes. We learned that Lucky Strike green had gone to war and was no more.

This small revelation was only the beginning of so many revelations that lay ahead for the eight* reborn souls speeding joyously toward the destroyer and a new world, free at last, indeed, from the rigors of World War II and the rubble of Rabaul.

September 7, 1945

* The seven long-term POWs plus newcomer, Ronnie Warren.

# FIRST EPILOGUE

I returned to the States on November 17, 1945 having been flown out of New Guinea to the Philippine Islands where I spent several days in the hospital at Tacloban and thence to Madigan General Hospital in Tacoma, Washington, and then to the Army hospital near Atlanta, GA in February 1946 and separated from the Army Air Force in August 1946. I married Mary Frances Smith in March '46 and pursued a civilian occupation until retirement in 1982.

Joe Holguin remained in the U.S. Air Force until eligible for early retirement as a Lt. Colonel; took post graduate courses in Education and became an assistant principal of a high school in Los Angeles. Joe was obsessed with the idea of returning to Rabaul, which he did on two occasions for the purpose of finding his crashed airplane and the remains of his fellow crew members. After forty years of rotting in the jungle about thirty miles from Rabaul, the plane was found and Joe directed the return of the ashes of his crew members to their families in the States.

Esco Palmer remained in the service and died in the early 1970's.

Joe Nason went back to Law School and served as legal council for a Massachusetts insurance firm until retirement. He and his wife then volunteered for the Peace Corp where he spent two years in a central Pacific island working in government affairs.

Bob Kepchia returned to civilian life as an employee of the U.S. Postal Service in Greensburg, Pennsylvania. He married and enjoys moderate health in his retirement.

Al Quinones rejoined his beloved wife Grace near Tucson, Arizona and for few years remained in quiet confinement until his interest directed him toward working with underprivileged Indian children near Mesa, Arizona.

John Murphy rejoined the Australian Government Services in the administration of the Mandated Territories. He became a district officer and served at several New Guinea posts including Wewak. In an effort to somehow reward the natives of Wageo Island who had so generously helped me and my crew, I wrote Murph in 1947 to inquire about how to send parcels to the natives on Wageo Island. Murph was stationed at the time at Higaturru and started his investigation by writing Father Ottenheim, whom he believed to be in charge of the Catholic Mission at Wewak some fifty to sixty miles from Wageo Island. Father Ottenheim was not stationed at Wewak and his letter was opened by Father Gerstner.

Gestner also wrote me giving news of the Wageo people and of the two terrible ship board massacres of the missionaries. Equally sad to me was the drowning of Mot and his son Lamouche.

Father Gerstner apparently took Murphy's letter addressed to Ottenheim to Kariru Island which is just offshore from Wewak and gave it to Father Meyer, who was in charge of the Kariru Mission with jurisdiction over Wageo and other outer islands. Gestner also delivered a letter to Father Meyer, which I had addressed to Father Ottenheim. He answered my letter of August 22nd and advised me on the type of gifts the Wageo people could most appreciate.

I again heard from Father Gerstner in a letter dated February 6, 1949. He described current conditions at Wewak and Kariru Island and informed "Wageo people" that I am alive and am sending presents to them.

On January 16, 1950, Father Meyer wrote me from Kariru Island saying he had received my gifts for the natives. Sadly he also reported the murder of old Maligum by the Manguma cult.

The Manguma cult referred to in Father Meyer's letter is a rite or custom of prehistoric origin. It focuses on vengeance. The "Tambaran House" or the "House of Men" where no woman is allowed inside, is a huge native structure housing masks and ritualistic art objects, ceremonial dress, etc. It is obvious that its collapse and with it the whole social structure it presents will be some day replaced by a church or by nothing at all. The ancestor worship will probably appear no more. Neglect, time, humidity and termites will finish off the rest. That is the high price New

Guinea must pay in order to enter into a new social order. In exchange, the western world offers a civilization that, despite the innumerable shortcomings of its laws and religions, undoubtedly has a power of persuasion that makes it, for the present at least, irresistible.

The missionaries, the politicians and the commercial interest will soon prevail and my indelible concept of a Melanesian culture will cease to exist. I am left with the enigma: will Wageo and the descendants of Mot and Maligum possess the innocence or the humanity to befriend an alien washed up on their 21st Century shore?

Father Meyer ultimately got his boat repaired and made the trip from Kariru to Wageo with my gifts to natives. I have neglected to mention that a contribution toward the purchase of these gifts was made by the surviving members of my crew: Leslie Burnett, Frank Wynne, Fred Engel and Bob Martindale, all of whom had been shipped out of Rabaul to Japan on November 13, 1943.

The good Father wrote me a glowing account of the reception he received on Wageo when he arrived with the parcel containing fish hooks, rope, cloth, tools of various types and cooking utensils. Unfortunately I have lost the letter describing their gratitude and their fond recollection of the strange Hamerikan who mysteriously appeared on their shore. Their inevitable and disquieting contact with the Japanese led them to believe that we had been captured and were beheaded; or if we reached interior New Guinea, we would have become victims of cannibalism. In any case, our survival was joyous news to them and the "sing-sing" in our honor was an island milestone.

## THE CAMPAIGN AGAINST RABAUL

On September 1946 a "Strategic Bombing Survey" was made and published by the U.S. Naval Analysis Division. This publication clarifies and expands the conception we POWs had with regard to the progress of the war, the conditions under which the Japanese garrison operated and their attitude toward military and civilian administration. The following are limited but significant excerpts from its pages:

"Japan began her carefully planned war against the western powers on December 8, 1941 (Tokyo time). Her attacks achieved almost complete surprise and in a short time the military, naval and air power of the Allies in Asia had been almost wiped out. The Japanese campaign of invasion and occupation were equally and successively victorious at Wake, Guam, the Philippines, Singapore, Hong Kong and Burma. The Japanese then turned their eyes toward what was to become for them their key base in the SW Pacific and the staging point for their projected encirclement of the Coral Sea--namely, the port of Rabaul." (pp. 5 & 6)

"In November 1943 total group strength around Rabaul comprised 97,870 men." (pg. 10)

"By July 1944 the Allies considered Rabaul's position was irrevocably lost and an invasion was unnecessary. For the rest of the war, however, a rigid aerial and naval blockage was enforced and diastematic bombing continued." (Pg. 17)

"The town of Rabaul was virtually obliterated by Allied strikes in the latter pat of 1943 comprising 990 buildings utilized by the Japanese as well as the air fields and port facilities." (pg. 27)

"By March 1944 most of the Japanese installations were underground. The Japanese had 350 miles of tunnels and caves, ranging from simple dugouts to labyrinthine facilities with timber-shored walls and supported roofs." (pg. 28)

"Unlike other by-passed Japanese areas, Rabaul suffered no serious shortage of food. Since the port was a receiving and distribution center for supplies, there were always large stocks on hand, and, after January 1944, supplies which would normally have been sent to Bougainville and New Guinea piled up here. To supplement these stocks, extensive gardens were planted and the yield of these was considerable." (pg. 34) "Both commissioned and enlisted personnel had occasional parties of a ceremonial and social nature. In the early phases of the war, 500-600 Japanese and Korean prostitutes were brought into Rabaul and a schedule was arranged which provided sexual entertainment for both officers and enlisted men." (pp. 34-35)

"Before the beginning of the war, the town of Rabaul had a population of 16,000-25,000 natives, 1,300 Chinese, 200 Malayans, 100 Europeans and a small number of half-castes. The Japanese assumed no real responsibility for the health of these people. Japanese handling of civilians was characterized by a callousness verging on brutality. Treatment of Chinese and Indian prisoners of war and of the Allied pilots shot down and captured was brutal in the extreme. Instances of torture, ceremonial cannibalism, execution for trifling or imagined offenses, medical malpractice and burials alive were revealed after the Japanese surrender of Rabaul." (pg. 35)

**Japanese atrocity**
(Photo courtesy Australian National Archives)

The McMurria family gets the good news.
L-R: Mary Gordy, John Henry (father), Henry Brooks
and Mary Brooks (mother).

MR.JOHN J.MURPHY
DISTRICT OFFICE
HIGATURU
NORTHERN DISTRICT
PAPUA NEW GUINEA

FR.GERSTNER
CATHOLIC MISSION
WEWAK
TERRITORY OF NEW GUINEA
10 TH AUGUST, 1948.

DEAR SIR,
AS THE FATHER IN CHARGE OF WEWAK MISSION STATION I
OPENED YOUR LETTER OF THE 19 TH JULY, 1948,ADDRESSED TO FR.OTTENHEIM.
HAVING NEVER MET FR.OTTENHEIM I HEARD ONLY THAT HE LIVES SOMEWHERE IN
BOGIA FAR FROM WOGEO ISLAND.IT IS A MATTER OF FACT NOT VERY LONG AGO I
HAVE BEEN ON THE ISLANDS WOGEO AND KOIL FOR A FEW DAYS.YESTERDAY I ALSO
MET 4 WOGEO-MEN HERE. IN WEWAK AND GOT A VERY GOOD INFORMATION.THUS I'M
ABLE TO ANSWER YOUR QUESTIONS.
BESIDES I REMEMBER WELL THAT GROUP OF 8 FLIERS,WHICH SPENT A TIME
ON KARIRU ISLAND AFTER CAPTURED BY THE JAPS ON THE MAINLAND AND LATER
SENT OFF TO RABAUL.MYSELF AND 11 MISSIONARY COMPANIONS,PRISONERS OF THE
JAPS,COULD EXCHANGE ONLY A FEW WORDS WITH THOSE FLIERS IN THAT TIME.FOR
THIS REASON YOU MAY UNDERSTAND ME ASKING YOU TO DO ME THE FAVOUR TO WRITE
DOWN THE ADDRESS TO LIEUT.J.A. MC.MURRIA ON THE ENCLOSED AIR LETTER AND
TO SEND THE LETTER OFF.MANY*THANKS FOR YOUR KIND-NESS.
THE INFORMATION I CAN GIVE YOU IS THE FOLLOWING.
THE OLD LULUAI MALIGUM A FINE MAN),HIS WIFE AND SONS ARE STILL KEE-
PING VERY WELL.MALIGUM'S OLDEST SON IS NOW IN CHARGE AS A LULUAI.
A PITY TO SAY THE "DOCTOR-BOY" MOT,HIS SON,7 OTHER WOGEO MEN AND
2 WOMEN WERE DROWNED ON A CANOE-TRIP FROM WOGEO TO THE MAINLAND AFTER
THE WAR.ALL PEOPLE AND THE CANOE DISAPPEARED WITHOUT LEAVING A TRACE.
MOT'S WIFE AND DAUGHTER ARE ALIVE.
THE HOUSES IN WHICH THE CREW LIVED WERE,FIRST MOT'S HOUSE AND THEN
MALIGUM'S HOUSE.
THE MEN WHOSE NAMES WERE MENTIONED FOR HAVING SUPPORTED THE CREW
WITH FOOD,ARE: SAWANG,FALTI,SABUG,WIUWI,ALL OF THE VILLAGE DAB.
THE 4 WOGEO MEN'S FACES BEAMED WITH JOY WHEN THEY RELATED OF"MASTA
JAMES",MASTA WIN",MASTA FRED",AND "MASTA SAGEN".

I HOPE THAT THE GIVEN INFORMATION IS SUFFICIENT.

WITH THE BEST OF GREETINGS
YOURS FAITHFULLY
FR.A.GERSTNER

LIEUT.J.A. MC.MURRIA                    FR,GERSTNER
"MASTA JAMES"                           CATHOLIC MISSION
                                        WEWAK
                                        TERRITORY OF NEW GUINEA
                                        10 TH AUGUST, 1948.

DEAR SIR,
          I HOPE YOU RECEIVED THE INFORMATION THROUGH J.J.MURPHY IN RESPECT
OF THE NATIVES ON WOGEO ISLAND,YOU ASKED FOR.IT WAS A PLEASURE TO GIVE
IT TO YOU BECAUSE I REMEMBER WELL THE 8 AMERICAN FLIERS ON KARIRU ISLAND,
FOR MYSELF WAS ONE OF THE IMPRISONED MISSIONARIES THERE.BROUGHT TO THE
ISLAND ON THE 13 TH MARCH 1943,THEN LIVING IN THE SISTERS HOUSE WITH
2 OF MY COMPANIONS FOR 10 DAYS(YOURSELVES WERE LODGED IN THE NATIVE HOS-
PITAL)WE HAD TO SHIFT TOGETHER WITH YOU TO THE PLACE OF THE CATECHISTS'
SCHOOL.DO YOU STILL THINK OF ALL THE HARDSHIPS REGARDING WORK AND FOOD
WE HAD TO ENDURE?YOU FLIERS ALL WITHOUT THE NECESSARY CLOTHING AND ALSO
WE MISSIONARIES HAD A BAD TIME,HAD'NT WE?BUT THANKS GOD,THAT'S ALL OVER
NOW.WE ALWAYS THOUGHT,AFTER WE HAD LEARNED THAT 4 AMERICAN FLIERS WERE
BEHEADED IN BAGARAM ON THE MAIN STATION,YOU ALL WERE ALSO KILLED.I'M
VERY GLAD TO HEAR THAT AT LEAST YOU ARE A SURVIVOR.BUT WHAT HAPPENED TO
THE OTHER 7 COMPANIONS?
          YOU ALSO CERTAINLY PITY THE NATIVE MOT(YOUR GREAT HELP ON WOGEO
ISLAND)AND HIS SON WHO WHERE WERE DROWNED BY AN CANOE-ACCIDENT.MOT WAS
THE MAN,AS I WAS TOLD,WHO DELIVERED YOUR MESSAGE AND GOT SOME MEDICINE
AND TRADE GOODS FROM THE AMERICAN PRIEST FR.MANION,ON KARIRU ISLAND.
WHEN THE JAPS LEARNED OF THE LETTER AND WHAT FR.MANION HAD DONE,HE WAS
IMPRISONED WITH ANOTHER BROTHER IN WEWAK AND I SUPPOSE,NOT WITHOUT GOOD
REASON,BOTH WERE KILLED THERE.
          AFTER THE JAPANESE POSITION IN WEWAK BECAME MORE SERIOUS IN CON-
SEQUENCE OF HEAVY BOMBING WE MISSIONARIES ON KARIRU GOT TRANSPORT TO
TUMLEO ISLAND,ABOUT 100 MILES FURTHER WEST,ON THE 8.11.43.THERE WE HAD
"HARD LABOUR"AND LESS FOOD FOR 5 MONTHS.
          THEN AGAIN ON THE 23.3.44 WE WERE LANDED ON THE SHORE OF HOLAN-
DIA.(DUTCH NEW GUINEA)FOR OUR GREAT SURPRISE WE MET IN HODEKAN THE REST
OF THE MISSIONARIES OF THE EASTERN VICARIATE,BROUGHT THERE IN FEBRUARY.
~~DREADFUL NEWS,56 MISSIONARIES~~,A BISHOP,PRIESTS,BROTHERS AND NUNS WERE
MOWED DOWN UNDER MACHINE GUN FIRE ABOARD A JAPANESE ~~SHIP BOUND FOR HO-
LANDIA~~.IN HOLANDIA WE ALL WERE SLOWLY STARVING TO DEATH TILL WE WERE
LIBERATED BY AMERICAN TROOPS ON THE 25.4.44.YOUR COUNTRYMEN ON THE IS--
LANDS AS WELL AS IN A BRISPANE HOSPITAL,RUN BY AMERICAN STAFF,TREATED
US GENEROUSLY IN ALL RESPECTS.
          ALL MISSIONARIES HAD A GOOD TIME DOWN IN AUSTRALIA BUT NOW
THEY ARE BACK IN NEW GUINEA AGAIN ON THEIR OLD POSTS EXCEPT A FEW SICK-
ONES.I RETURNED IN SEPTEMBER 1946 AND HOPE THAT ANOTHER 20 YEARS WILL
BE GRANTED ME AFTER HAVING BEEN ON THE MISSIONES FOR 21 YEARS ALREADY.
          WHEN WE WERE SHIFTED TO TOMLEO ISLAND THE FATHERS MAY AND REIF,
2 OF OUR COMPANIONS,WERE KEPT BACK ON KARIRU ISLAND AND BEHEADED LATER
FOR THE REASON THAT THEY KNEW A LITTLE OF WHAT THE JAPS HAD DONE ON THE
MAINLAND.
          AS A RESULT OF A WAR-CRIMINAL-COURT IN RABAUL IS NOW KNOWN,THAT
BISHOP LOERKS OF KARIRU ISL.,TOGETHER WITH OTHER 58 MISSIONARIES,WHO
HAD TO LEAVE THE ISLAND ON A JAPANESE SHIP ON THE 15 TH MARCH 1943,WERE
TIED TO THE SHIP'S RAILING,SHOT DOWN AND THROWN INTO THE BILGE WATER
OF THE SHIP.
          THUS OUR MISSIONES,A COUPLE OF PEOPLE WHO DIED OF SICKNESS AND
STARVATION INCLUDED,LOST 120 PERSONS DURING THE WAR.PRACTICALLY ALL MISSI-
ON-STATIONES WERE DESTROYED,IN WEWAK AND ON KARIRU ISL.TOTALLY.
          BUT WHY DID I TELL YOU ALL THESE BAD NEWS?YOU MIGHT BE INTERES-
TED IN ISLANDS ON WHICH YOU SPENT A CERTAIN TIME.
          ON THE MISSIONES THERE HAS NEW LIFE STARTED AND IS GROWING AGAIN.
AFTER THE WAR 36 AMERC.PRIESTS CAME OUT ALREADY AND WE ARE WAITING FOR
ANOTHER 24.TO REPLACE OUR 2 KILLED BISHOPS 2 AMERC.PRIESTS WERE APPOIN-
TED NEW BISHOPS 3 WEEKS AGO.
          AND NOW "MASTA JAMES"AND MYSELF 'LET US CHEER UP,FOR WE ARE STILL
ALIVE AFTER THIS HORRIBLE WAR.YOUR LIFE WAS SAVED BY THE BLACKFELLOWS
AND MINE BY THE KIND AND GENEROUS AMERICANS.
          WISHING YOU THE VERY BEST FOR YOUR FUTURE,I REMAIN WITH
          ALL KIND REGARDS
                    YOURS FAITHFULLY
                              FR.ANDREW GERSTNER.
                              F. Gerstner

WEWAK,FEBR.6,1949.

DEAR MR.JAMES A.MCMURRIA,

MANY THANKS FOR YOUR KIND LETTER OF NOV 29,1948,WHICH I RECEIVED NOT LONG AGO. I'M SORRY FOR NOT HAVING BEEN ABLE TO ANSWER IT AT ONCE. MEANWHILE I MET YOKEO PEOPLE IN THE HOSPITAL AGAIN,RELATED THEM OF WHAT YOU WROTE TO ME.THEY WERE VERY MUCH DELIGHTED TO HEAR OF YOU,THAT YOU ARE KEEPING WELL AND HAVE NOT FORGOTTEN YOUR OLD FRIENDS.ALSO BLACKFELLOWS CAN BE FAITHFUL.---FR.MEYER WHO GOT A LETTER FROM YOU RECENTLY,OWNES A SMALL MOTORBOAT AND IS VISITING THE ISLANDS EVERY SECOND MONTH OR SO NOT MANY OF VOKEO PEOPLE ARE CATHOLIC BUT WE HOPE THAT MOS OF THEM HAVE ACCEPTED THE CATHOLIC FAITH AFTER A FEW YEARS. THOSE PEOPLE ARE RATHER SECLUDED FROM THE OUTWORLD BUT THEY SEEM TO BE HAPPY ON THEIR BIG ISLAND.

I THINK YOU STILL REMEMBER KARIRU ISL.VERY WELL.LAST WEEK,ON THE WAY TO TUMLEO,ISL, I SPENT A DAY AND A NIGHT THERE.AN AMERC FATHER AND A GERMAN BROTHER ARE REBUILDING THE OLD ST.XAVIER'S SCHOOL NOW.THE SLEEPING HOUSE DOWN CLOSE TO THE RIVER,WHERE YOU AND YOUR COMRADES HAD TO CARRY HEAVY STONES BARFOOTED AND BAR- HEADED, IS ALMOST FINISHED.THE WELL NEAR THE HOUSE,YOU HAD TO DIG, IS FALLEN TO RUIN.HALF THE HILL,WORK ON THE SCHOOL BUILDING, HAS NOT STARTED YET.THE FORMER HOUSES AS WELL AS OTHER BUILDINGS WERE COMPLETELY DESTROYED DURING THE WAR,EXCEPT THE FRAMEWORK OF THE SMALL HOUSE,WHICH.A FEW JAPS USED AS A SLEEPING ROOM AND DINING ROOM.THIS HOUSE WAS RECENTLY FIXED UP AND THE FATHER IS LIVING IN IT.ON THE BISHOP'S STATION,WHERE YOU WERE SHELTERED IN THE NATIVES' HOSPITAL,A DUCH FATHER,ABOVE MENTIONED,IS IN CHARGE OF A PARISH.HE HAS A CHURCH-BUILDING ALREADY,BUILT OF BUSH MATERI AL,AND A POOR HUT FOR HIMSELF.THIS? I SUPPOSE MIGHT INTEREST YOU. WEWAK IS DIFFERENT FROM PREWAR-TIME.BEFORE THE WAR IT HAD A POPULATION OF ABOUT 30 WHITES TODAY MORE THAN 80 WHITES LIVE ON THE HILL.THE OWNER OF A FREEZER IN WEWAK POSSESSED A CAR AND TH MISSION ANOTHER SMALL TRUCK,THAT WAS THE LOT OF ENGINE VEHICLES BEFORE.NOWADAYS JEEPS AND TRUCKS,QUITE A FEW DRIVE ALONG THE MIS ON-STATION. AND MORE MILES FAR TO THE EAST AND ABOUT 10 MILES TO THE WEST.THE MAIN ROAD IS IN GOOD CONDITION BUT THE BRIDGES WILL ALWAYS GIVE MANY DIFFICCULTIES.ONLY A SOLID IRON-BRIDGE ON CONCRETE PIERS CAN STAND THE HIGH TIDE OF A NEW GUINEA RIVER.

SHIPPING IS STILL VERY POOR AND THERE IS NO ONE OF A SHIP, COMING FROM THE SOUTH,EVERY 8 WEEKS AS IT WAS BEFORE THE WAR. MAIL SERVICE ALSO IS NOT VERY SATISFYING FROM MY HOME COUN- TRY,WESTERN GERMANY, I RECEIVE A REGULAR LETTER AFTER 4 OR MORE MONTHS.

AIR CRAFT IS THE RIGHT THING FOR NEW GUINEA.I THINK THE AUS TRALIANS ARE DEVELOPRING A FEW AIR-LINES, NOW WEEKLY WE HAVE COMM NICATION WITH MADANG,LAE AND AUSTRALIA.FLYING SEEMS TO BE MORE DIFFICULT IN N.G. THAN SOMEWHERE ELSE.THERE WERE 6 PLANE-CRASHES DURING THE LAST 5 MONTHS.ALSO OUR MISSION LOST 2 PLANES(DRAGONS NOT LONG AGO.A PRIEST, PILOT WAS KILLED.

IT IS A PITY THAT TILL NOW I COULD NOT GET THE ADDRESS OF FR.MANION'S RELATIVES.

I HAVE NO WANT OF MISSION WORK.AFTER TOMORROW I GO BUSH FOR A FORTNIGHT.MANY JOYS AND PLEASURES HAVE BEEN MY LOT DURING A MISSION LIFE OF MORE THAN 21 YEARS NOW.YOURSELF ALSO KNOW THE CANNIBALS OF N.G.NOT ONLY FROM HEARING BUT BY EXPERIENCE.HOW ARE THEY?--WISHING YOU GOD'S BLESSING,I REMAIN WITH THE BEST OF GREETINGS

YOURS FAITHFULLY

FR.A.GERSTNER

*Fr. Gerstner.*

# SECOND EPILOGUE

After James (Jim) McMurria's death in 2003, friends and family continued to inquire about his war experience story, which he had reluctantly recorded in a small book entitled *Trial & Triumph*. When a military historian, Ed. Y. Hall, pursued an interest in his book in the summer of 2005, the family decided to publish the story on a larger scale. *Fight for Survival* is the result of that effort. None of the original text has been altered.

Mary Frances, Jame's wife of 56 years, recalls a series of unusual coincidences that occurred during his journey home from the war. After his rescue by the Australian navy, he was taken to a hospital in the Philippines where he struck up a friendship with an American soldier. This young man, from Greenville, S.C., had worked for Mary Frances Smith's father and was engaged to Mary Martin, a friend of James' in Columbus, Georgia. From the Philippines, James was taken to a hospital in Tacoma, Washington and was immediately recognized by another soldier who exclaimed, "I thought you were dead!" It was Martindale, Jame's co-pilot who had been one of the 35 prisoners transferred from the Rabaul prison camp to Japan.

After an "unofficial" hospital release, Joe Holquin and James hitchhiked to Los Angeles where James caught a military plane to a base in Washington, D.C. In the Washington office, he found a soldier reading the Columbus, Georgia "Ledger-Enquirer" whose headlines chronicled the survival and rescue of James McMurria!

James married Mary Frances Smith on March 2, 1946 and, against the prediction of his physician, he and Mary Frances had four children and, eventually, seven grandchildren. After a long career in textiles and banking, he retired from South Carolina National Bank in 1982. The following year, 5 of the original 7 POW camp survivors met for a reunion at the McMurria home in Greenville, S.C. Their reunion and the story of their survival was published in *Parade Magazine* in September of 1993.

A woodworker, gardener, writer, outdoorsman, community

volunteer and lifelong tennis player, James was nominated and selected to take part in the running of the Olympic Torch prior to the 2002 Winter Olympics.

In September of 1995, at the invitation of President Bill Clinton, James was awarded the POW Medal presented by the Secretary of the Army, Togo West, in Honolulu, Hawaii. This was part of the National Commemoration of the 50th Anniversary of VJ Day.

Until his death, James remained in contact with his fellow survivors and crew. He hosted a reunion of the 90th Bomb Group (H) 5th Air Force, in Greenville in August of 2001 where General Paul Tibbetts was the featured speaker. After a long and fulfilling life, this remarkable "soldier" died on August 5, 2003.

Mary Frances Smith

**Wedding Day – March 2, 1946**
**James and Mary Frances**
**Greenville, South Carolina**

**The McMurria Family**
**Left to right: Brooks, Harriet, Austin, and Anne**
**Seated: Mary Frances**

# A QUESTION OF
# SURVIVAL
## BY  LARRY  SMITH

'WE'RE GOING IN! WE'RE going in!"

The pilot, Lt. James McMurria, and his crew of nine, carrying four 1000-pound bombs on their B-24 Liberator, had come east over the Owen Stanley range on the spine of New Guinea that morning, Jan. 20, 1943. As they reached the Japanese port of Wewak on the coast of the Bismarck Sea, more than 20 Zeros scrambled to meet them. The Zeros were almost twice as fast as the B-24. McMurria dropped two bombs and headed for a cloud bank out to sea.

But the clouds weren't thick enough to hide in, and the Zeros swarmed around the bomber. They shot out two engines and damaged the controls, so McMurria had no choice but to ditch. He was 60 miles offshore. As he set the plane down on the rolling sea, it broke in half and began to sink.

McMurria shoved his pilot's window back. Already under water and craving air desperately, he kicked to the surface. Fred Engel, the radioman, cried out for a knife—the life raft, tied to the sinking plane, was going down. Tom Doyle, the bombardier, dug out of his pocket a key ring with a jackknife on it and threw it across several feet of ocean to Engel, who caught it with his one good arm (he'd hurt the other tearing himself free), opened the blade with his teeth, dived down and cut the raft free. Four men climbed in and four clung alongside as they hurriedly kicked away from the suction of the sinking plane. Shortly, one of the two bombs on board blew up.

For 2½ years after that day, no one heard a word directly from McMurria. Yet, at the end of August 1945, he was one of only seven men to walk out of a Japanese prison camp. Why did those seven live and so many others die?

Jim McMurria today is 66. He retired a year ago from his job at a bank in Greenville, S.C. He smokes, he takes a drink, he's had trouble with ulcers. He lives with his wife in a red brick house with a magnolia tree in the yard. They have three daughters and a son, all col-

*Survivors of a Japanese prison camp, September 1945: (Left to right) James McMurria, Alfonzo Quinones, Jose Holguin, Escoe Palmer and John Kepchia.*

lege educated. It sounds simple enough, but Jim McMurria knows things only experience can teach, and I went to Greenville to ask him about a few of them. I had read of his ordeal in an account of a reunion held a few months before. I was very interested in learning what extraordinary talents, if any, what special resources, had enabled him to survive. Might we learn secrets for our own survival from a man like James McMurria?

The raft the crew had salvaged as the B-24 went down was torn apart on the coral when, on their second night at sea, the crew risked going ashore on an island called Vokeo. "We

*The prisoners recalled songs, wrote up recipes, made cards from cigarette packages ...They held on.*

were," recalls McMurria, "turned upside down, scattered, we hit coral and suffered a lot of shock. We were sunburned, thirsty and cut by coral, but we were on dry land. What a relief."

Fred Engel, who lives in Texas now, remembers that a wild pig trod on him that night and that he awoke in the grasp of a native with bushy hair and a bone in his nose and he was terrified, he says, until the man inquired, "Drink, master?" Engel laughs. "He was so gentle, holding my head up just like a nurse, he was—and so ugly."

Several weeks later, on a beach in New Guinea, following a similar landing after their outrigger canoe had overturned, the crew again awoke to strangers. But this time they were Japanese soldiers, about 25 of them, and, McMurria recalls, "they came in screaming."

Despite being barefoot and in tattered clothing, the fliers had hoped to make their way up the Sepik River, over the Owen Stanley range and down to Port Moresby on the southwest coast of New Guinea. McMurria still toys with the idea. As it was, he and the others ended up in a hole in the ground at an enemy camp a few miles north. Here, they underwent their first interrogation.

When McMurria's turn came, he was ushered into a little room and made to kneel with his hands tied behind his back. The officers sitting at the table began asking questions through an interpreter. McMurria signaled for paper and a pencil. His hands were freed and he wrote down name, rank and serial number. With a smile today, he recalls how the four officers studied the writing and, finally catching his drift, they burst out laughing.

A guard was called, and he came over and began stomping the prisoner. "Luckily," says McMurria, "he was wearing tennis shoes." After a while, the prisoner managed to inform the officers that there had been a "misunderstanding," that he was happy to answer questions. The beating stopped, the interrogation resumed and, says McMurria, he tried to mislead his questioners.

After being moved several times, the crew was locked up in a Chinese tailor shop in the city of Rabaul, a major Japanese port. Here, in a series of rooms and in darkness—including three days spent handcuffed and jammed standing in a cave—the ordeal of the downed airmen spun itself out through hunger, illness and death. Four crewmen of the bomber, including Fred Engel, were taken to a camp in Japan and survived the war. McMurria's bombardier and two other of his crewmen and eight others were called out of the cave one night, taken away and presumed shot.

*continued*

At one point, the number of prisoners at Rabaul rose to 78. Seven survived to the end of the war. A year ago last summer, five of these men got together at McMurria's home in Greenville. They try to keep in touch.

The obsession in Rabaul was with food, which consisted of rice balls, sometimes a pineapple and bullet-hard biscuits. Once in a while, a sympathetic Korean cook would throw potato peelings to them in the dark through the 2-by-4 bars of their cell, and all would scramble on their knees for the slivers.

When Allied bombers dumped crude oil, then came back with napalm and destroyed the vegetable gardens in Rabaul, the prisoners got no rice for six weeks. They contracted malaria, scurvy, beri beri and tropical yaws. They developed sores open to the bone, and many of them died. Others were executed.

The fliers were constantly finagling to add to their diet, entertaining their guards with "circuses," anything to get a little biscuit, a candy ball, some rice or a smoke. The guards called McMurria "Fred Astaire" because he could do a soft-shoe. He also harmonized with another prisoner on the hymn "In the Garden." Another prisoner could recite "Casey at the Bat." They fashioned cigarettes for the guards with a homemade roller and were given cigarettes for pay.

To pass the time, the prisoners made a deck of cards out of Japanese cigarette packages, they wrote up recipes, they talked about movies, books, songs, everything. They were given one 828-page volume, covering letters H through M, of the *Chambers Encyclopedia*, published in Australia in 1895. They read every word, and everybody wrote in it. McMurria has it to this day.

Escape was impossible, says McMurria. Rabaul was on New Britain, an island containing 86,000 Japanese, and "there was no place to escape to." The prisoners tried exercising at first, and there were work details, but as weakness and sickness set in, there was nothing left except to hold on or die.

At one point in his captivity, at the invitation of the Japanese, McMurria wrote a deceptively positive letter home, which Tokyo Rose read over the radio. Her words were picked up by a listener in India and, on Jan. 12, 1944, he wrote to McMurria's parents that their son was alive and a prisoner.

This was the first word to reach the States since he'd been shot down a year before. McMurria's lady friend at the time, Mary Frances Smith, recalls that when word came, "it was just thrilling."

At Christmastime of that year, McMurria's body grew so bloated with fluid that death seemed certain. There was a tree next to the cell, he says, and he began nibbling at the leafy shoots. "The swelling went away," he says. "I think

that saved my life."

When a bloated, sickly man began to "bite the air," says McMurria, the others knew he was going to die. The Japanese respected the dead and allowed religious ceremonies. The prisoners told their captors that, by their custom, when a man died, food was left by the body while the living smoked cigarettes and prayed and said good things about him. From that time on, when a prisoner died, the guards would provide a bowl of rice, which the survivors put at his head, a pineapple, which they placed at his feet, and cigarettes, which they smoked. They were men of different faiths, and the services were mixed. McMurria is a Presbyterian, but to this day he rattles off a Hail Mary with ease.

"We hated to see anybody die, naturally, but as soon as the natives took the body out," he says, "we'd go for the food. We tried to be decent, but we were starving to death."

To what, then, does James McMurria attribute his survival in the Pacific? He speaks of luck, mental toughness and a strong constitution.

"I can't put my finger on any one compelling reason," he notes. "I think patriotism had little to do with it. My death would be of no significance to either America or Japan." As for trust in God, he says that everybody prayed and that "there were many who died who I felt had a stronger faith than mine."

Mainly, he declares, "I did want to live. A few of the prisoners actually didn't because of the severity of the conditions coupled with their weakness from disease. They gave in to a sense of hopelessness. The Japs insisted the war would last for a hundred years. With very little information to go on, I felt there was a chance that they might be right. It was a lousy feeling."

I had set out to discover something about the mysteries of survival under extraordinary circumstances, to meet an unusual person of extraordinary capacity. What I found was this: In order to become somebody special, you first have to learn that you are like other people, and this was something Jim McMurria had known long before he was shot down. I asked Fred Engel not long ago what he thought of McMurria, and he said, "I loved him. I still do. He always took care of you."

What I found in Jim McMurria, then, was no more than a man, a very good man. And that is his strength.

At the end of my visit, he told me: "Some have said that God intended me to live for a specific purpose. I have not found that purpose other than returning to a normal existence, marrying Mary Frances, the wonderful girl with whom I was in love at the time, and enjoying the rewards of raising four fine children, for all of which I feel very lucky and grateful." 🔲

The Greenville News 1 Sept 1995

# Ex-POW is front and center again

*Jim McMurria is to accept a war medal in honor of WW II's end*

By Ron Barnett, Staff Writer

As much as he's tried, Jim McMurria can't keep history from knocking on his front door. The retired Greenville banker has been asked so many times to account his tale of torture and starvation at the hands of the Japanese during WW II, of being shot down in the Pacific and living among aboriginal island inhabitants for months before being captured, that he dreads dredging up the topic again.

"I don't want to sound like I'm bellyaching," McMurria said. But with Saturday marking the 50th anniversary of the day the treaty ending the war in the Pacific was signed, McMurria's story is in demand.

He's been asked to accept the Prisoner of War Medal from the Secretary of the Army today in ceremonies at Pearl Harbor, where President Clinton and other top U.S. Military leaders will gather this weekend to celebrate V-J Day.

The event is the climax of a five-year commemoration of WW II sponsored by a presidential commission, an army official said.

McMurria, now 77, was chosen to receive the medal after his story came to the attention of Secretary of the Army Togo D. West Jr., a spokeswoman for the secretary said.

"Secretary West wanted to be able to do something during the ceremonies in Honolulu to honor Mr. McMurria and his service," spokeswoman Dawn Kilpatrick said.

McMurria downplays the honor.

"I'm going out there not to get some sort of medal," he joked. "I'm going out there to have a big time."

He can laugh about it now. But 50 years ago, after being injected with malaria-infected blood and watching two of his friends die from the disease just two days before the Japanese surrender, he was still awaiting liberation while the world celebrated the treaty that ended the war.

His ordeal had begun nearly three years earlier, on Jan. 20, 1943, when, as a B-24 pilot flying his 20th reconnaissance mission with no fighter protection, his plane was surrounded by a group of Japanese Zero's and shot down off the shore of New Guinea.

"If I was going down in a plane today, I'd scream and holler," McMurria said. "But it didn't bother me too much then. I thought, 'We'll work it out somehow.'"

The plane broke in half as soon as it hit the water. Two of the ten man crew did not survive the crash. "When I got out of the window I must have been 40 feet under the water," McMurria said.

One of the plane's two life rafts didn't eject like it was supposed to, forcing four of the eight survivors to cling to it's side as they paddled and swam for three days and two nights before making it to an island. There they befriended the natives and lived about two months before deciding to try to make it back to their home base 600 miles away in Australia – by canoe.

They hopped nearly 200 miles from island to island with the help of the natives before arriving at New Guinea. But there, they were betrayed, lashed to poles and imprisoned in a 12 foot hole in the ground.

Later, during Allied bombing attacks, they were crammed into a cave so small they had to stand for three days.

"We were starved to death, beaten, deprived of any Red Cross packages," McMurria recalled. "No sanitary facilities whatsoever. No clothing. No beds. No bomb shelter."

The food at the camp in Rabaul, a Japanese stronghold on the coat of New Britain, was so scanty that McMurria's weight dropped from about 180 to under 100 pounds. Only seven of the nearly 80 POWs who were there at one time had died as the end of the war approached.

And then came the medical "experiments."

A Japanese doctor, seeking a clue as to why the Americans seemed to have greater resistance to malaria than the Japanese, drew blood from five of the remaining seven prisoners and injected them with Japanese blood infected with malaria. Two of McMurria's comrades died days later. McMurria credits his survival to having developed some resistance to the disease through numerous previous infections.

On Sept. 7th, 1945, five days after the surrender was signed in Tokyo Bay, the Australians liberated the camp. But before he left, the Japanese, "for some reason," paid their captives, McMurria recalls with a grin. He remembers exactly how much he "earned" for his years of suffering – 1,635 yen. (That's after deductions for "food and lodging.") In today's exchange rate, that would amount to about $16.50. In 1945, it was probably worth closer to $3.25, McMurria estimates.

"That's a dollar a year," he laughs.

Though he's reluctant to acknowledge it – citing the suffering and death of thousands of others during the war – perhaps history owes him a bit more than that. And, after 50 years, the bill comes due this weekend in Hawaii.

**James Austin McMurria receiving Prisoner of War Medal from Assistant Secretary of the Army, Togo D. West.**

**Olympic Torch Runner – 2002 Winter Olympics**
**James on the left with fellow runner and friend, Jack Cromartie**

# The Greenville News

*Greenville,*
*South Carolina*

THURSDAY, AUGUST 7, 2003 ■ FINAL EDITION

greenvilleonline.com

**Weather**
Chance of showers and t-storms in the afternoon.
High: **85°**
*Details, 6B*

## 'Real hero' James McMurria dies

### Greenville man was WWII prisoner

**By Abe Hardesty**
STAFF WRITER
ahardest@greenvillenews.com

James McMurria, who spent nearly three years of his life as a prisoner of war and the last several as a civic volunteer, died Tuesday at Greenville Memorial Hospital.

At 85, complications from pneumonia took the life of a man who loved making contributions — without fanfare — to others.

"He was a real hero in so many ways," said Nancy Renn, Greenville Literacy Association program director. "He was a perfect example of what volunteerism is all about. It's a very sad day here at the Literacy Association; we've lost a real ambassador and a great human being."

**GreenvilleOnline.com**
■ For coverage of the 90th Bomber Group reunion at Donaldson Center, go to GreenvilleOnline.com

In his retirement, the former accountant and banker was a near-daily volunteer at the GLA, where he tutored in the English-as-a-Second-Language program and, until a recent illness, sorted books that will be used in an upcoming fundraiser. McMurria, who enjoyed woodworking as a hobby, served as co-chairman of that committee.

"He was wonderful for our organization," Renn said, "but we'll miss him even more as a person. Every time he came in, he shared a thought or a joke or an idea. He was a joy to be around."

McMurria, a lieutenant and pilot in the 90th Bomber Group, flew 20 com-

*See* **HERO** *on page 4A*

**'Very lucky':** James McMurria was an Army lieutenant and pilot in the 90th Bomber Group, at left. During World War II, he spent nearly three years as a prisoner of the Japanese. Recently, he was a tireless worker for the Greenville Literacy Association. The photo at right was taken last year.

# HERO

FROM PAGE 1A

bat missions in the Pacific in late 1942 and the early days of 1943. But on Jan. 20, 1943, his B-24 bomber was shot down off the coast of New Guinea.

McMurria was among five of the 10-man crew that survived the plane crash in the Pacific but was eventually captured and sent to Rabaul, a prison island where hundreds of Americans were squeezed into small, hot, crowded wooden structures that housed disease and starvation. When McMurria left the island on Sept. 7, 1945, following the Japanese surrender, he was among seven prisoners who had survived.

In his book, "Trials and Tribulations," McMurria printed his diary, which chronicled the ordeal and the men who shared it with him. He was also the subject of a 1983 Parade magazine article on the horrors of Rabaul. In 1995, as part of the anniversary observance of V-J day, McMurria received a Prisoner of War Medal "symbolizing the courage you showed and the hardship endured by you and other American soldiers" during the POW experience. In a ceremony at Pearl Harbor, McMurria represented all American POWs of the World War II era. And in 2000, he was selected as one of those who carried the Olympic torch as it passed through Greenville.

But for most of his life, McMurria was reluctant to discuss his military contributions.

In refusing two *Greenville News* requests in the past year, McMurria declined to be the subject of a story "because I'm not a hero. I was sitting in prison while the real heroes were charging machine-gun nests."

Many friends never knew of McMurria's POW experience. "He never talked about it. Over the years, I was able to squeeze out some things, because I was persistent and because we shared an interest in history," said Jack Cromartie, who played tennis with McMurria twice weekly until the past month.

"You hear about real American heroes, but it's not very often you get to know one. I know that other military men were more decorated ... but Jim never promoted himself," Cromartie said. "He was for real — there was not a phony bone in his body. He was ornery and honest, and you always got a kick out of being around him."

Cromartie, the former Community Foundation president, said McMurria once told him of his POW confinement, "You'd never understand unless you've experienced it — so why talk about it?"

Cromartie attended an August 2001 reunion of five surviving members of the 90th Bomber Group, and sensed an unusually high level of respect for McMurria. "Every one of the others told me they'd go anywhere with Jim McMurria. It was apparent that he had been their emotional leader."

A Georgia native and University of Georgia graduate, McMurria came to Greenville shortly after the war and worked as a banker and accountant. He

as a banker and accountant. He married Greenville native Mary Frances Smith, whom he had met while stationed at Donaldson Air Force Base shortly before he was sent to the Pacific. In 1942, as Donaldson AFB was under construction, McMurria was the first pilot to land a plane there.

For a year after his plane was shot down in the Pacific, his wife and parents knew only that he was missing in action. In January 1944 McMurria wrote a deceptively positive letter home, which was read over the air by Japanese propagandist Tokyo Rose. It was heard by a listener in India who wrote to McMurria's parents to inform them that he was alive.

For the next 58 years, McMurria often wondered why — and felt a sense of guilt — that he survived while others did not. A Presbyterian who says he prayed daily as a POW, McMurria said, "There were many who died who I felt had a stronger faith than mine."

In the September 1983 Parade article, McMurria described a postwar life of fulfillment in "a normal existence, marrying Mary Frances, the wonderful girl with whom I was in love at the time, and enjoying the rewards of raising four fine children, for all of which I feel very lucky and grateful."

# Rabaul POW Camp Statistics
# 1942-1945

There were 126 "known" Allied prisoners:

- 91   Americans
- 28   Australians
- 6   New Zealanders
- 1   British

of these known prisoners:

- 67   Were executed
- 19   Died in captivity
- 20   Missing – status unknown
- 20   Survived the war

On March 5, 1944, the Japanese Kempe Tai
executed 35 Rabaul area POWs.

The above list does not include civilians
(planters, missionaries and other personnel) being held
by the Japanese at Rabaul, New Britain.

Source: *Seige At Rabaul,* by Henry Sakaida